GRAND SLAM

COACH YOUR MIND TO WIN
IN SPORTS, BUSINESS, AND LIFE

ANNE SMITH, PH.D.
WITH SCOTT EDWARDS
AND BEV GAY-RAWS

FOREWORD BY BILLIE JEAN KING

GRAND SLAM: COACH YOUR MIND TO WIN IN SPORTS, BUSINESS, AND LIFE

Published by Team Alf Books
Phoenix, Arizona

Photo Credits:
Russ Adams (Front Cover)
Bev Gay-Raws (Back Cover)

Additional Resources by Anne Smith:
MACH 4 Mental Training System™: A Handbook for Athletes, Coaches, and Parents (book)

ISBN 0-9778958-1-5

Visit Anne's website at www.annesmithtennis.com
Email Anne at anne@annesmithtennis.com

DEDICATION

I dedicate this book to my parents, Dr. and Mrs. John Lee Smith, my sister Sue Smith Ross and my beloved brother Roy Lee Smith. Thank you for supporting me all the way. Roy, we all miss you.

ACKNOWLEDGEMENTS

I would like to acknowledge the following people for assisting me in the creation of this book: Bev Raws for her insightful and intuitive contributions; Team Alf for their inspiration, guidance, and support; my friends Marc Gearin and Masako Nakamura, whose friendship and help has been priceless; my friends George Warshaw and Stephanie Ellis, for planting the seed and giving me the confidence to write this book; Bunny Williams and Missy Malool, USTA Tour Supervisors, for their wisdom, encouragement, and help; USTA/ITF tour players who welcomed me back and inspired me to keep playing; Billie Jean King, a true pioneer whose vision and courage led the way for me and all female athletes to reach their dreams; Martina Navratilova, who has inspired everyone to pursue their dreams no matter what the odds might be; Scott Edwards, who took all of Bev's and my ideas and made this book a reality; and last—but not least—AJ and Spike.

GRAND SLAM
COACH YOUR MIND TO WIN IN SPORTS, BUSINESS, AND LIFE

FOREWORD

BY BILLIE JEAN KING

The way each of us approaches challenges in sports, business, and life changes as we get older, more experienced, and actually get a chance to live and learn life lessons. But, those who possess the great gift of being able to see the big picture and be a big player are the ones who lead us forward. Anne Smith is one of those people.

In her new book, *GRAND SLAM: Coach Your Mind to Win in Sports, Business, and Life*, Anne provides us with a personal, insider's perspective on competing. Rest assured, Anne is a competitor—and we all know you don't get to be number one in the world in anything if you aren't. She provides us with several key insights in this new book. But most importantly, Anne reminds us that in order to achieve greatness you must focus on the things you are doing well and make them even better. This approach gives you the skills and the attitude that ultimately allow you to rise above the competition.

Anne Smith, if she is anything, is adaptable. This adaptability allowed her to win ten Grand Slam doubles and mixed doubles titles with five different partners. I always played my best with those partners who could make me laugh and Anne definitely made me laugh. She called me "Tree Trunks" because of my short legs. I called her "Tree Trunks, Jr." even though in her playing days her legs were definitely smaller than mine. We kept each other calm on the court and that allowed us to communicate better. And there was a type of unspoken radar between us that kept us in the match. By listening and communicating we played better tennis, won tournaments, and truly enjoyed a great day at the office.

As a tennis player there are always many people who want to get in your head. From coaches, to parents, to business advisors, to your competitors, everyone has an opinion to share. Tennis, like so many sports, requires as much mental strength as it does physical power. Champions come from those who understand that knowing what to do and when to do it is as much a part of the game as knowing how to do it.

Near the end of my playing days I arrived at the 1983 Tournament of Champions in Orlando, not expecting to play doubles, and Anne asked me to partner with her that week. I did it on one stipulation: we needed to win the tournament. Anne looked at me in a bit of disbelief because Martina Navratilova and Pam Shriver were the top seeds in the draw and they had a 40-match win streak heading into the event. We didn't kid ourselves; it was a big hill to climb. But we believed in ourselves and in our plan, and when the final was over, we had upset the champions, 7–6 (11–9) in the third set. We won one for us. After that, Martina and Pam went on to win 109 consecutive matches, a record that still stands today. But what Anne and I pulled off on April 24, 1983, will always be one of the more memorable moments in our collective careers. Without us, Martina and Pam's record would have been well over 150 consecutive match wins.

If you are a coach, parent, athlete, business leader, or someone who wants to make a difference, Anne's book will speak to you. Take to heart her motivational messages, learn from her personal stories, and allow yourself to enjoy what lies ahead for you.

Billie Jean King
May 2006

INTRODUCTION

Dreams do come true! My dream began when I was 12 years old, kneeling down on Centre Court at the All England Lawn Tennis & Croquet Club and taking a few pieces of that precious grass, then turning to my family and saying, "I'm going to play here some day." Call it intuition or just plain desire; I knew that I would some day play on that majestic court during Wimbledon.

I was lucky. My parents believed in my dream and made it possible for me to have my chance. My parents only asked one thing, no matter where I played: I was to represent my family well. The endless practicing and training paid off in 1977 when I walked onto Centre Court at Wimbledon ready to play one of my idols, Billie Jean King. As I sat and looked around at all of the spectators waiting to see me play one of the greatest players of all time, I could not help but bend over and touch that grass again just to make sure that this was real. My dream had come true! Imagine, I was only 17 years old, playing my first Grand Slam, Wimbledon, and I was through to the second round to play against Billie Jean King. Incredibly, I won the first set 8–6. What a feeling! I did not win that match, but what an honor to have been able to play three sets against such a great champion.

Even today, people often ask me what the best moment in my career was. I always tell them that it was when I won my first Grand Slam doubles title with Kathy Jordan at Wimbledon in 1980. The feeling of lifting that trophy in the Royal Box on Centre Court is indescribable. Now at age 46, I am continuing a comeback in professional tennis that I started in February 2005. I look back on my career and that moment, and I really know that dreams do come true. It is exciting to know I am beginning a new one.

Vince Lombardi did not say, "Winning isn't everything. It's the only thing." What he really said was, "Winning isn't everything, but the *will* to win is." This book is about how to win—in sports, business, and life. Winning, we all know, is not only about the score at the end of the game. That is important, but so is putting yourself in a position to win, empowering others to win, being a positive role model, being a good teammate, having fun, learning new things, and taking risks. These themes pertain not only to sports but also to managing employees and nurturing relationships as well.

How do I know about winning? From the time I was a teenager, I was among the most talented tennis players in the world. When I was 17, I was the first American ever to win the French Open Junior Singles Championships. Between 1980 and 1984, I won ten Grand Slam championships in women's and mixed doubles, including three U.S. Open titles, two Wimbledon titles, four French Open titles, and one Australian Open title. I am one of only 20 women in the history of the Open Era of tennis (1968 to present) who have won ten or more Grand Slam titles. I was ranked #1 in the world in women's doubles in 1980 and 1981, and was ranked as high as #12 in the world in women's singles. I played with and against some of the greatest names in the history of tennis, including Martina Navratilova, with whom I won the French Open doubles championship in 1982 in addition to five other WTA tour titles.

With this successful past, why would I want to make a comeback? Because my passion and love for the game is still there. I also do not want to look back ten years from now and ask myself why I did not try. Many times we do not go after our dreams because of a fear of what others might think or say. Believe me, I do not like losing, but the greatest loss of all is not trying. This time, however, I am doing it differently. I have given up the idea that I cannot miss, or that I have to be perfect. During my career in the 1980s, my perfectionism fueled my anger and caused me to feel as if I were fighting myself instead of my opponent. But I have now learned how to manage this perfectionism and anger by encouraging myself and by focusing more on what I am doing well.

On the International Tennis Federation (ITF) pro circuit, where I am playing singles and doubles, young women are working to make their dreams come true, too. People have asked me why I don't just play doubles. It is because playing singles is a bigger challenge. It also enables me to meet more players so that I can find a doubles partner. Besides, my highest singles ranking was #12 in the world and that's not bad! Even though I won three singles titles, I firmly believe that if I would have had the MACH 4 Mental Training System (read more about this in chapter 11) when I first started playing tennis and used it throughout my career, I would have won many more.

Unlike now, I never had to play on a "Futures" tour or in the qualifying draw because my ranking always allowed me to enter in the main draw on the main tour. I equate this to never missing a cut on the pro golf tour. Now, for the first time, I have to play in the qualifying draw at some of the current tournaments.

The game has changed significantly since I last played competitively, in 1991. There is more of an emphasis on power now, although when I played against Monica Seles, she could hit the ball as hard as any of the current players. But the game is about so much more than hitting the ball!—all of these young women can hit the ball well. It is about the mental part of the game. This is where I benefit from what I learned studying for my Ph.D. in educational psychology, and putting it into practice as a school psychologist working with children, teachers, and parents. I have had to create a mindset that allows me to compete with players who are 20 or more years younger. These players work on the physical part of the game, but they seldom work on the mental part. Most players do not even realize that it is possible to develop a tougher mental attitude, much less know how to do it. As I have said to some of the players, "It's just like practicing a backhand down the line." Mental toughness can be learned. I learned it, so I will share with you how you can become mentally stronger, which will enable you to win more often.

On this tour, I have seen many negative interactions between coaches/parents and players. It is very disheartening to hear coaches and parents speak in a harsh and derogatory manner to their players—their sons and daughters. They also foster dependent relationships, which do not instill self confidence, self discipline, or self motivation. Time after time, I see players looking to their coaches or parents after every point. This does not create a winning environment. This type of support to a player just creates more stress and more reasons to lose. The job of a parent or coach is to find the best ways to enhance the players' performance. Through experience I know that a harsh, critical approach does not work. It leads to self doubt, anger, illness, and injury. Players need a strong, supportive team to help them maximize their performance.

If I were a parent, I would not allow a coach who does not take a positive, supportive approach to influence my child. Children often put their coaches on a higher pedestal than even their parents. Don't parents want the best role model to teach their child how to win? I was lucky to have had two positive coaches at the beginning of my career. Imagine: I was able to learn the strokes that were right for me and allowed me to win 13 national junior titles without being berated or humiliated by a coach or parent. Every child deserves to have a nurturing environment as they try to make their dreams come true.

Too often today, the emphasis is put on who wins and who loses—as if the score was all that mattered. Dignity, integrity, and sportsmanship are often tossed aside in the quest for victory. Players, coaches, and parents often lose sight of why games are played. Everyone wants to win, and there is nothing wrong in that. But the extent to which people will go to win is alarming. We hear about parents who are involved in violent confrontations with coaches over their child's lack of playing time, or of coaches physically or emotionally abusing players whose ability or effort does not meet their expectations. None of this creates a winning environment.

With this book, I want to help players, coaches, parents, employers, and employees—and others—develop a prescription for how to win. If you are a coach or a supervisor, you will learn effective strategies for creating a positive environment and enhancing the performance of your players or employees. If you are a player, you will find effective ways to reach your maximum potential and put yourself in a position to win—and at the same time have fun and learn new ways to win. If you are a parent, you will find ways to identify potentially destructive negative behavior in the ones who coach your children. You will also be able to develop healthy, positive relationships with your children and their coaches that foster a winning environment.

GRAND SLAM also includes my life experiences. You know the saying, "If only I knew then what I know now, I would have done things differently." For me, I would have not been so hard on myself and others. I would have realized how critical it was for my words and actions to be more positive and empowering. My successful tennis career could have been accomplished much easier with a different mindset. I could have celebrated and enjoyed my wins more. I would like to share these life experiences with you so that you know it is possible to look inside yourself and to make constructive changes. I have been able to make changes that have made me a better and happier person. The good news is that people can change, no matter their age or what has transpired in their life. It is easier than you think; I am a good example.

For anyone who has enjoyed the thrill of athletic competition, there is no better feeling than walking off the court or playing field after a victory. The will to win is part of human nature (this is a part of Darwin's theory of survival of the fittest), but, unfortunately, the forces that prevent us from winning—negativity, sarcasm, domination—are also part of human nature. The next time you are near a ball field, tennis court, or other athletic facility, take a look around. Observe the behavior of the players, the coaches, the parents, and the fans. That behavior will tell you, regardless of the score, who is winning and who is losing. I believe in the power of positive training and coaching to win. By the time you finish this book you will also.

CHAPTER 1

ALLOW YOURSELF TO WIN

You cannot win unless you allow yourself to win. That means creating an environment in which you *can* win. It means surrounding yourself with people who help you win—coaches, trainers, teammates, teachers, supervisors, co-workers, and friends. And it also means instilling in yourself—and others—a positive attitude that reinforces winning and success.

On the other hand, a negative environment creates a barrier to winning. It is said that negativity breeds contempt. Well, it also breeds losing. If the focus is always on the negative—from a coach, a parent, a boss—then one is not allowed a sense of how to win. That negative feedback will only teach one to be negative, rather than focusing on what is positive about the performance. Negativity is unproductive and unnecessary. It only creates more stress and anxiety, which is not part of a winning formula. Sometimes I think people believe that if they are not hard on someone, that person will not achieve. That is the furthest thing from the truth. Focusing on the negative creates a vicious cycle that I have seen time and time again. If a player has been coached and/or parented negatively, that player will not allow herself to win and will often "choke" when games get close. Is it possible that on some subconscious level, the player is getting back at her parent or coach by not winning? If this is the case, is negative coaching worth the risk?

Art Faust, Jr. was my first tennis coach, starting when I began playing at age 11. He coached me for nearly four years and, as he said, "...took me as far as he could." He was a persnickety coach—very exacting but not harsh. He never yelled at me or degraded me. He created a positive environment in which I could learn the game of tennis—and win. When I left Mr. Faust, Danny O'Bryant became my coach. Danny transformed my game, changing my strokes and adding a loop backswing to my forehand. He was a calm, positive influence on me and my game. Once again I was fortunate; my early coaches were positive.

However, this was not always the case. Growing up in Texas, I was always #1 in my age group, as well as the next older age group. I was easily beating other girls, but the focus was often on what I did wrong. There was one person who, if I had won a set 6–1, 6–0, focused on what I did to lose that one game, rather than on what I did to win the other 12. I certainly did NOT enjoy that type of feedback. But again, I think it was the mentality that you always have to tell someone what they did not execute well rather than just saying, "You played great," and celebrating the win. For many young kids, consistently focusing on what they are NOT doing creates a strong negative picture in their minds. The mind will repeat what we give the most feeling and energy to in our thoughts. The word "mistake" becomes too easy to say and to think about. How about the words, "I executed my shots well"? When we train our minds to take those words to heart, realizing that we may need to continue to polish our skills, we can take many more wins home with us rather than, at times, giving them away.

As a recovering perfectionist, I fed into that attitude. Throughout most of my career, I focused my attention on what I did not do well. I was my own worst enemy. I often did not enjoy playing because I was so hard on myself. How many times do we see players come off the court asking what they did wrong? It seems that people have more difficulty when someone compliments them rather than when someone critiques them. Now when I receive a compliment, I say "Thank you" and allow my mind and body to receive that feedback graciously. In the past, as I achieved my goals, I never even took a moment to appreciate them or experience joy from what I had accomplished. I was continually raising the bar. How many of you fall into that category?

Today, I look at compliments as nourishing my mind and body. This new way of thinking and acting has created many joyful, wondrous events in my life. Whenever I dwelt on negative aspects, I experienced loss, illness, and injury in my career. As I look back, I remember key moments when I was at the top of my game and an illness or injury would sideline me. I got food poisoning at the French Open as I was cruising in singles to the quarterfinals and had to default. I contracted mumps at Wimbledon after getting to the quarterfinals of the singles and winning the doubles and mixed doubles titles. With all of the information available today that emphasizes the importance of the mind/body connection, why would anyone want to have an input of negativity?

Since I am older—and wiser—I realize that this negativity takes too much energy, and in the end is not helpful or enjoyable. I still have high standards for myself, but I am trying to back off a bit and focus more on enjoying the game and improving rather than on what I am doing wrong, or on winning and losing. This has really made a difference in my comeback. I am enjoying the competition, whether I win or lose. It is not the end of the world anymore if I lose. In the past, losing would affect my play in future matches. Now, I focus on each match separately and stay in the present rather than dwell on the past. No matter how much thought and energy we spend on lamenting past events, the outcome never changes. It is best to keep looking forward and, as much as we can, not be tempted to keep looking back.

Unfortunately, many of today's coaches do not see things this way. Most coaches today are too intense—in every sport and at every level. They prowl the sidelines, berate players and officials, and stare in contempt. I would rather watch the athleticism and beauty of the sport than players and coaches acting out during games. Sports have gotten way out of hand. A lot of the interaction between player and coach today is negative— some of it even vulgar. You may create a champion that way, but at what cost? In fact, if a coach creates a negative environment, it may come back to bite him. Kids will not want to play for a coach who is predominantly negative. Players who deal with negativity on a regular basis will not be able to perform when it is needed most— at those crucial times in a contest when belief in self is all important. As their muscles tighten and their heart rate increases, the player's focus and risk taking decreases. Likewise, employees do not want to work for a supervisor who is always critical and never offering positive feedback on a job well done. Unfortunately, the negative attention many of these players and employees get is *all* the attention they will ever get.

When I look into the eyes of some of today's young tennis players, I see fear as they come off the court because they know they will be yelled at by their father or mother, who wants to know why they did this, why they did that. Parents can put too much emotion into winning and losing rather than maintaining some distance from the emotional aspect of it all. It is obvious when a parent is living vicariously through their child. When this happens, the parent and his feelings become the center of attention rather than focusing on what is best for the child. Their child certainly did not *want* to play poorly, but sometimes that happens. Many parents have no idea what it takes to create a champion. Parents and coaches should be looking to enhance physical skills that will join with the mind to allow improved performance to take place. Being negative and overly emotional does not accomplish this. In fact, more stress is created.

When a coach and/or parent is predominantly negative, they need to take a look at themselves and figure out why they are acting that way. Believe me, it has nothing to do with their son's or daughter's performance and everything to do with something inside of them. Parents and coaches want their player to perform well. When I watch matches, however, I often hear, "Why did Judy do that? Why is she doing that again?" If you are a parent watching your child play, or a coach on the sidelines watching, are these the types of comments that you are thinking or making? If so, this is a red flag! Just sit back and watch the match. A coach or parent is there to lend full emotional support and energy to the player competing. Whatever the result, the most important aspect is how that coach or parent talks with the player after the match, rather than whether the player won or lost. On the ITF tour, I have seen coaches make derogatory comments about their players in front of other players and coaches. They have told others that their player just flat-out choked. Of course, that gets the coach off the hook immediately, as if he had nothing to do with it.

Coaches and parents have everything to do with it. A young teenage player came off the court in a recent pro tournament after losing a three-set singles match leading 5–3 in the third set. Her mother asked, "Why did you lose that match?" The player responded, "Because I always choke when I'm ahead." The question is who created this mindset and how? From what I have heard about this young player, her father's negativity certainly had something to do with her belief system.

When someone is constantly critiquing me or reacting to my missed shots, I become even more frustrated. I get angry and lose sight of why I am playing: for the love of the game. One of my hitting partners was like that. If I missed a shot, he would make a comment or just stare at me.

I certainly did not need that. Besides, who does he think he is? Coaches need to be very careful how they interact and respond to their players. Negativity breeds anger, resentment, and failure. Players who are subjected to this kind of coaching or parenting will eventually seek ways to get back at the negative coach or parent. So when the score is close, the player may choose to lose in order to do this. Why would any coach or parent take a chance on this happening?

A constant focus on what your player is doing wrong only reinforces those thoughts in her mind. Players then become afraid they will make "mistakes" instead of feeling confident in their shots. How can anyone think that berating a child (or another adult) can produce positive results? For someone to allow himself to win, he needs to think that he deserves to win. If there is any doubt about this at all, it will show up on a big point. Players cannot overly focus on technique during a match; they have to go with the flow and play on instinct and learned behavior. If they are thinking too much about technique and a coach's critiques, the focus becomes more result-oriented rather than letting the winning just happen. The more someone forces—often the result of negativity—the worse the result may be.

A better approach is to teach players how to accept compliments and positive feedback, turn it inside, and use it to win. Then, at the end of the match, players are happier about their win, and can actually accept the fact they *have* won. Often players compete and hardly appreciate the actual win, acting almost as if they *should* have won. When I look back on my career, I did that. I expected to win, so I never really enjoyed the win as much as I could have—and should have. Now when I win a match on the ITF tour, I really celebrate it and feel good about myself.

Many of today's young tennis players have developed unhealthy, codependent relationships with their coaches. Seeking constant attention— even negative attention—they look over to their coaches after every point. When I see this, I know there may be a problem. Players need to be self-motivated and independent. They cannot achieve this if they are constantly looking to the sidelines for reinforcement and approval. Unlike other sports, tennis coaches are not permitted to "coach" during matches. However, instruction does occur as these young players seek this implicit feedback—and some of it is negative. Coaches must allow players to think for themselves and make those crucial decisions when the game is on the line. When coaches do the player's thinking for them, they create a tension that leads to increased pressure—and that impacts a player's ability to win. The competitive arena is a different plane; you have to love the pressure. If a player is supported in a positive, learning environment, he will adapt to this pressure. You need confidence to want to be the player with the ball at the end of the game, to take that last shot. Confidence in these situations only comes from the atmosphere in which a player is reared. If the atmosphere is negative, the player will, more often than not, not come through successfully. If the environment is positive, the player's chances of success are much greater.

Coaches must focus on what is right with a player and build on that. Comment on the positive: "I like the way you did that." Correct misses by saying, "I'd really like you to try…" This heightens the player's interest and creates a positive learning environment. As a tennis instructor, I have a distinct philosophy of teaching. It is a system in which things are phrased differently in an attempt to create a safe environment for learning. I encourage my students to learn new shots, to try new things, and to take risks. A good way to do this is to catch them making a good shot or making a shot they have been working on, and then immediately complimenting them. This is so much more motivating than harping on what the player did not do. Many players are good enough and aware enough to know when they have messed up; they do not need to be told that by a coach. Coaches need to know what brings out the best in their players, not the worst. This can only happen in a positive, safe environment. My students beam when they execute a shot and get praised for it. In this environment, they become better players and enjoy the game more. And, they keep coming back for lessons!

I have seen how this philosophy has helped my recent comeback in professional tennis. Because the game has changed so much since I was at the top back in the 1980s, I have had to learn new things to adapt to the modern game of tennis. I could never have done that in an environment that produced anger and negativity. Bev Raws, my current coach, has created an environment in which it is safe for me to learn, to take risks that will allow me to continue to improve, and to win. It is a fun environment, with a lot of energy. Believe me, she has made all the difference in the world. I could not have made this comeback without her. Her positive coaching philosophy has allowed me to continue to compete on this tour without getting completely discouraged. She has focused on what I have done well each match and built on that. She has made small adjustments along the way rather than completely overhauling my game. I have added new shots without losing what I already had in my game.

We have discovered that the techniques and mental strategies that made me a champion are still inside of me, and they are beginning to appear again. In fact, we have begun to realize that the way I played in the early '80s is what is helping me win some of my doubles matches now. I am chipping and charging—and the opposing players hate it! Also, Bev introduced a concept that a winning shot or well-played point is worth 20 points, and a miss is worth only one point. This "trick" puts the focus on the positive and minimizes the negative. It has made a big difference with me. I am starting to "blow off" any misses that I make and to get excited about playing well even if I do not win the point or match. It is okay for me now when I come off the court after losing. I know that Bev will see the positive in my play no matter the score. This philosophy has helped me to play better.

The key to creating this environment is to know your audience. What is reinforcing for one student may not be reinforcing for another. As a coach or supervisor, you need to know how your players and employees will learn best. I am a visual learner, so I need less dialogue and more demonstration. My father once told Danny O'Bryant, my childhood coach, "Don't *tell* Anne how to hit a forehand, *show* her how." I have noticed more and more that most players have short attention spans and are easily distracted. So when I am teaching, I keep my comments brief. I also look for differences in players' responses to their misses. I often find that some players are their own worst critic, and after missing a shot will turn to me and ask, "What did I do wrong?" They do not need a coach reinforcing their self-criticism, so I generally say, "You missed the shot and it's only worth one point." Special care has to be taken with children, especially, for whom everything—positive and negative—becomes the truth. Children cannot perceive an adult's sarcasm; they internalize it, creating their own self-negativity. They cannot win that way. Somebody—the coach or parent—has to step in and stop this type of negative interaction so that the child can feel better about herself, not worse.

Negativity can also ruin the dynamics of a team. As the saying goes, "One bad apple spoils the whole barrel." If even one player on a team is drenched in negativity—from a coach, a parent, a teammate, or himself—the whole team can become infected with this negative vibe. Teamwork (which I address in chapter 6) is a partnership among players and coaches, employers and employees, teachers and students, and parents and children. Our responsibility as a member of a team is to be a good partner to our self and to everyone on the team.

Part of allowing yourself to win is creating realistic expectations. If your expectations— or those of your coach, employer, parent, or teacher—are too high, you may never be able to succeed. For me, it was unreasonable to expect that I would win my first matches in my comeback. However, I went into those tournaments thinking I could win a match right away. Boy was I wrong! I had to make adjustments. I had been out of competitive tennis for 14 years. I needed time to reintegrate myself to the professional game, including much-needed match play. These players had been competing and playing on this tour for years. Why did I—or anyone else for that matter—think that I could come in and start winning right away? In fact, I lost the first three singles matches that I played. After these tournaments, I went back and looked at some of the players' records on the ITF tour just to get an idea of how they had worked their way up in the rankings. I found out that these players had started at the lowest prize money tournaments in the qualifying rounds and some of them had not won a match the whole year. Why should I not be allowed the same leeway as these players? So I had to adjust my expectations for myself. I went from focusing on winning a match to focusing on winning points. This mental change has made all the difference because it has helped me stay more in the present. The trick is to not allow yourself to have a mindset that points are cumulative. Once a point is over, it must truly be over. The next point is brand new and not related to past points. That way the mind can then play each point as if it is new and separate from what has just occurred.

Right now, for me, winning has nothing to do with the score and everything to do with how I feel about myself and my game. Don't get me wrong: I want to win, but I must be patient and keep competing if I am to be successful. Because I have set reasonable expectations, I have already won. I have shown that I can compete against women who are 20–25 years younger. Because I feel good about myself and my game, I allow myself to win. This is the winning part of winning.

CHAPTER 2

EMPOWER OTHERS TO BE GREAT

Everyone wants to be the quarterback. But not everyone can, or should, play that position. Part of creating a winning atmosphere is empowering others to be great, regardless of their position on the field, in the classroom, or in the corporate hierarchy. One way to do this is by putting players and employees in positions for which their skills are best suited and where they can use those skills for the team's benefit while feeling good about their own performance.

A friend of mine coaches Pop Warner football. At the first practice of training camp, he and his fellow coaches ask, "Who wants to play quarterback?" Almost everyone raises his hand. Needless to say, a team made up entirely of quarterbacks is destined for certain failure. So after the team has been divided into positions, my friend, the offensive line coach, gathers his players, many with their heads down because they have not been assigned one of the so-called "skill" positions. He tells the kids, "You see those guys over there—the quarterbacks, receivers, and running backs? They can't do anything without a line in front of them. You are the engine that drives this train."

What he is doing is making them feel that they have an important role in the team's success; he is empowering them to be great. What the linemen do enables the backs and receivers to perform well, and the backs' and receivers' performances are a reflection of the linemen's play.

Everyone on a team is important. Everyone has an important role to play—from the star who scores the most points to the last player on the bench who provides moral support and encouragement to his teammates. This is the essence of a team: working together toward a common goal and performing your job to the best of your ability so that your teammates can do their jobs well also.

In my doubles career, my job was to set up the point so my teammate could put the shot away.

My role was to set up an aggressive partner who loved to poach (come to my side of the court to intercept a shot), which I did not like to do. By letting Kathy Jordan poach and hit winning shots, I empowered my teammate to be great. Together, we won Wimbledon and the U.S. Open, French Open and Australian Open doubles titles. We each had a role, and we each did our job well. To this day, I wear my WTA doubles "Team of the Year" medallion, just so I do not forget what can be accomplished when two people enable each other to be great. Of course, there were times when I would have liked to have been the "star" instead of the "back-up singer." But if I had let my ego take over, I really wonder how many Grand Slam titles I would have won.

Now, my role is different. I am counting on my younger partners to set me up so I can make the winning shot. I am the one who has to take advantage at the net because of the way players are playing doubles now. Most of the players are more comfortable staying on the baseline, so I am always at the net, looking to poach whenever the opportunity arises. I have completely changed my mindset in doubles. I am more aggressive, and I love to poach now. I never thought I would be a good net poacher. A change in court movement and believing that I could do it have given me a better game and a new, aggressive style that I love. Do not believe that old saying, "You can't teach an old dog new tricks"!

Coaches, supervisors, and other leaders play an important role in empowering those under them to be great. This creates a team concept and a positive, winning attitude. How teammates interact with one another is critical to a team's success. It is up to the coach to manage that interaction by fostering an environment in which everyone feels important.

This is especially true in sports; however, the same rules apply at work and in the classroom. If you, as coach, create the team, then everyone on the team *should* be on the team. Some coaches allow kids to be on a team when they are not really ready. It is always difficult to say no to someone who wants to be on a team. Ask yourself: Is allowing this child to be on the team in the best interest of the child? Is it not our job as coaches to have the best interest of each child at the heart of our decisions? Ultimately, this critical decision will either create a winning environment for the team or more frustration for coaches, players, and parents. Which environment do you wish to create?

Most youth sports programs have minimum play requirements to guarantee that kids, while not necessarily getting equal playing time, do not just sit on the bench during games. The rule may say that a player may only sit out one inning each game, or that they must play ten plays or so many minutes each game. These rules create an environment in which each player is important to the team's success because he is in the game for a certain number of plays, yet they allow coaches the flexibility to put players in at key times during the contest so the team is in the best position to win.

Coaches creating ways to inspire players to keep coming back to play—and playing, even if it means a minimum number of plays—is one step toward this goal. Another way is to compliment players in a positive manner. For players whose skills are not on par with some of their peers, a simple "You're doing great, keep up the good work" goes a long way in making the player feel that he is providing something valuable to the team. Each player—or employee or student—is different. Each learns from the other.

When I was coaching the professional World TeamTennis Boston Lobsters during the 2005 season, there were times when players were either not getting to play in matches at all, or were only playing in one set. Of course, every player wants to play every match, so if a player was not upset about sitting on the bench, I would have to question that. When a player is not playing as much as he would like, his behavior and reaction become critical not only to him but to the team environment.

During the Lobsters' season, I received a lot of feedback regarding the players' demeanor on the bench. This was valuable information that allowed me to see how the fans perceived the players' behavior. I used this feedback during individual and team meetings. I told players who did not get to play very often how important they were to the team and that it *did* matter what they said to their teammates and how they conducted themselves on the bench. I also stressed that I wanted them to look good, whether they were playing a little or a lot. How they conducted themselves on the bench was a reflection on all of us. I was trying to empower them to be great regardless of their playing time. The result was that every player had an active role in helping the team to victory. We were a true team, which, as you know, is sometimes difficult to achieve and sustain.

Another key element of empowering others to be great is for players to have trust in the coach's decision making. Implicit in that trust is that the decisions made are for the benefit of the team, rather than any individual. Coaches can ensure this trust by believing in and telling their team that they are not just the coach, but that they, too, are a member of the team. This attitude and leadership certainly promotes more camaraderie and fun while achieving the primary goal: winning!

As coach of the Lobsters, it was my job to fashion a winning team. This was important to the owner, the city of Boston, and the team itself. I had to make the critical order of play (deciding which sets to play first, second, third, fourth, and fifth) and the lineup decisions for every match. My decisions were not always popular, but it was my responsibility to create a winning environment regardless of whether my decisions were popular or not.

There were times during the season when I asked for player feedback, particularly regarding the order of play. I welcomed the team's input; however, I was the one that made the decisions regarding the lineup. For example, if I saw that one of my players was playing better than his partner in doubles, there was a good chance that I would substitute the person who was playing better that night into the mixed doubles. These substitutions were not always understood, but I was considering the best interest of the team, enabling each player to contribute in a necessary and meaningful way. Everything turned out well, as the Lobsters made it to the playoffs as a first-year franchise. We won a playoff spot by edging the Philadelphia Freedoms by ten games. Everyone on the team contributed to winning those crucial games. Would Martina Navratilova have played in the last five matches of our season if she did not love the team and its contagious chemistry and spirit? She proved how much she enjoyed playing for the Lobsters. She played in our last important regular season match for free. How many professionals would have done that!

At the professional level, it is the coach's job to produce a winner, and decisions that are made must always be in the best interest of the team. In our case, we were able to have it all—a trip to the playoffs, a winning team spirit, and players who were empowered to be great.

CHAPTER 3

CREATING A WIN-WIN SITUATION

Most people become involved in sports because they want to get something out of it. Players want to learn, to get better at their sport, and to win. Coaches want to continue to be involved in the games they played, to share their knowledge, and to win. The same can be said in business, in school, and in relationships. These are not zero-sum relationships in which someone's "win" must be matched by someone else's "loss." In order to be successful, a win-win situation must be created in which all parties involved can benefit.

In sports today, that win-win situation—or quid pro quo, or whatever else you want to call it—is getting lost by people who are too invested in the score at the end of the game. The focus is on "getting mine," not working as a team. The thinking goes something like this from the player's perspective: "If I lead the team in scoring and we lose, they can't blame me." From the coach, the thinking goes like this: "All I can do is coach; I can't play the game for them." In neither of these situations is there a winner—despite the score at the end of the contest.

Coaches—and players—must realize that sports are not a life-and-death situation; no one is going to die if they lose. Coaches who feel that sports are life-and-death create anxiety and tension among their players. They demand—not ask—things from their players, creating a negative environment in which no one can perform to the best of his ability. This type of coach turns the game into a competition between coach and player instead of focusing on competition against the opponent. Thus, no one learns, and no one wins.

Let me illustrate how damaging a situation can become when that win-win focus disintegrates. During my recent comeback, I had the opportunity to hit with a very well respected instructor. Our first hitting session was fun, and I learned a lot. It was the beginning of a real win-win situation for both of us. Then the bottom fell out.

This instructor began to get controlling; he was abusive, berating, and condescending. He began to put the misses back on me rather than helping me correct what I needed to change. The tone of the hitting session had changed. In his mind, he was now in charge and the remainder of the session would be conducted his way, with little thought or concern about what I wanted or needed to learn from the session. In the end, this session produced discouragement and anger, and left me wondering why a good coach would speak to a player the way he spoke to me. The trust was gone, so the only thing to do was to end the relationship. The win-win focus changed when this instructor lost control of his emotions and determined what was best for him rather than what was best for both of us. There is no excuse for the behavior I experienced that day. Creating a win-win situation means understanding not only what you want to learn from a certain situation, but what others want and need as well. This means understanding yours and others wants and needs and finding a solution to meet both ends.

From the coaching end, win-win situations begin with positive dialogue and good two-way communication. Coaches need to ask their players (or managers-employees, teachers-students, parents-children) what their goals are as individuals and as a team, and then create an environment in which everyone works toward reaching those goals. This can also help a coach set realistic expectations for his team. If a coach's goal is to win the division championship, but the players' goals are to better their record from the previous season, then a serious disconnect exists. The coach will push his players a certain way to achieve *his* goal, while the players will take another set of actions to reach *their* goals. While acting toward the coach's goal may help the players reach theirs, and vice versa, this does not ensure that either side will win. Had the coach discussed his goals with the team and allowed them to talk about theirs, a compromise—and thus a win/win situation—could have been reached. I recently asked the juniors that I am coaching to let me know whether they wanted to be in the top 1,000 in the world or the top ten. Based on their answers, I told them I would coach them accordingly. They all said, "We want to win Grand Slams and be in the top ten." My response to them was that they must train like Grand Slam champions to become Grand Slam champions. Their training habits immediately began to change. This type of dialogue created a win-win for both the players and the coach.

When a win-win plan breaks down, the environment changes from asking certain things of players to demanding things from them. In a nutshell, this is what many of today's athletes experience with over-demanding coaches and parents. The players become subservient to the demands of the coach or parent, creating a climate of control and dependency rather than allowing the player to function independently and think for himself.

This type of environment creates negative energy, which keeps people from performing at their top level. Players who get caught up in this type of environment just wait for the next negative comment to come. They tighten up, force misses, and suffer even more demeaning behavior from their coach or parent. Being treated this way produces nothing but self-doubt and fear, and, as we all know, fear produces non-optimal performance. Steve Cauthen, the youngest Triple Crown winner in the history of horse racing, did a television commercial with me in the late 70s for Trident Sugarless Gum. This is what Steve has to say about fear: *Anybody who says they have no fear is lying. But you can't be afraid and ride successfully. You have to overcome it, mentally. You also have to be athletic, ambidextrous, and able to make split-second tactical decisions in the midst of thundering iron-clad hooves and thousands of pounds of muscle, with no protection but goggles and a helmet.* This highlights the negative impact of fear. Knowing how critical it is to overcome fear and self doubt in competition, why would parents and coaches choose to contribute to these negative energies? Kids have very little control in these situations—but coaches and parents most certainly do.

My experience with the tennis instructor I mentioned earlier taught me what kids must feel like when coaches berate them; it brought back a flood of memories from earlier times in my professional career when coaches were controlling, selfish, and demanding. Their excuse that it "makes the player tougher" is *so* far from the truth. I would much rather train with someone who is fun and respectful, and helps me elevate my game, rather than with someone who creates anxiety and fear. What about you?

Most kids put their coach on a pedestal. Anything the coach says is "God's word." Coaches must realize the psychological impact they have on their players, especially young ones, with their behavior. A coach can be positive and encouraging, or he can be negative and demeaning. How he acts toward his player is a choice he makes. The son of a friend of mine decided that he never wanted to play T-ball again because his coach had yelled and screamed at him. I recommend that parents attend one or more practice sessions to ensure that their child is not receiving that type of coaching. The risk of negative coaching is more than just having athletes who never want to compete again. This behavior changes who they are; it gets to their soul and impacts their lives far beyond the playing field.

All coaches have a great responsibility for both their players' physical *and* emotional well-being. We must create an atmosphere in which both the coach and the players are winners. I know that what I say to a player will either make her stronger or make her weaker. I want to make her stronger by encouraging her and making sports fun and rewarding to play. Creating this type of environment also helps to keep the athlete's mind engaged longer in the activity. Time seems to go by much more quickly with less energy expended. A player I recently worked with in Scottsdale had this to say after our practice session, "I felt so calm when I was hitting. I didn't feel like I had to force my shots which always makes me feel more pressure. I had fun, learned new shots, and felt like I had a lot of energy left over." I felt the same way. I also enjoyed the session and hardly noticed the 100 degree heat! For me, it is so rewarding to watch a player perform without fear and play with love and a passion for the game. If we as coaches and parents create the best environment for learning and performing, then we are winners also!

CHAPTER 4

DIALOGUE AND DELIVERY

Coaching sports, at all levels, is about dialogue and delivery—knowing what to say, when to say it, and, most importantly, *how* to say it. As an old adage goes, "It's not what you say; it's how you say it." This is never truer than it is with coaches, especially those involved in youth sports.

There are three generally accepted styles of coaching, each of which lends itself to a certain manner of communication. The first is the Command Style. This is the "do as I say" approach to coaching, with the coach as dictator or autocrat. Coaches who employ this style want to be in total control—of players, of officials and, at the college and professional levels, of the media. They also want to win at all costs.

Command-style coaches are often the ones you see in abusive situations. I see this in tennis, especially when a man is coaching a young woman or girl. He ends up sometimes being more than just her coach. Command-style coaches' dialogue is usually negative, harsh, and critical. Bobby Knight, the celebrated Indiana basketball coach who is now the coach at Texas Tech, falls into this category. He has such incredible knowledge and skill that he could translate to his players in a much less stressful manner, for him and his players. Yet he yells and berates his players for the smallest "mistakes." In his earlier days at Indiana, he is alleged to have physically attacked players—even throwing a chair across the court in a fit of rage. Is this really needed for players to perform their best? If so, I would like to ask the players if they really need that type of emotional coaching for inspiration and motivation. If that is what it takes to perform well, count me out! A coach must teach, inspire, and be a strong role model, not a bully.

Regardless of the command-style coach's ability to teach, again I ask, "Is this type of coaching really necessary to win?" Isn't this behavior more about the coach's inability to control his emotions than what is really going on with the player? I know that I have to manage my emotions to win, so why do coaches think they do not? The command-style coach is certainly not a good role model for the young athletes who watch or are on the receiving end of this behavior.

Another coaching style is called the Submissive Style. This is a style in which the coach offers limited or, in some cases, no instruction. There is no structure to drills or practice sessions. Players make the decisions, rather than the coach. Coaches adopt this style for a number of reasons, including a lack of ability to effectively instruct athletes, a lack of confidence in their role as a leader, or the fear of reprisals from players, parents, or administrators. I have seen coaches who allow their teams to practice with low intensity and not be good practice partners to their teammates. I have also seen team captains partake in this behavior, as the coach is reluctant to demonstrate strong leadership. These coaches try to please everyone; however, this approach just causes more disruptions and distractions.

The third style is the Cooperative Style. With this approach, the coach allows his athletes to become involved in decision making and gives them part ownership in the team and its future. Because they are so involved, athletes under cooperative-style coaches are more easily motivated. When I was young, my coaches had a calm manner about them. They were not sarcastic or demeaning; there was no aggression in their approach. My current coach, Bev Raws, is in the cooperative-style camp. We have effective two-way communication. We value each other's input and work together as a team. With this approach, my game has become stronger much faster and easier.

One of the biggest and most important aspects of these coaching styles is the ability to communicate. Command-style coaches often yell and use negative language. Submissive-style coaches use very little communication because they are not in control. Cooperative-style coaches use words of encouragement, positive feedback, and two-way communication with their athletes.

Coaches can be better communicators by making certain that their actions match their words. If you are in a frenzy on the sidelines and then tell your players to be calm, your actions do not match your words. The result: more stress and anxiety. The team may still win, but at what cost to you and your team?

There are a number of ways that coaches can become better communicators:

- **COMMUNICATE WITH PLAYERS AS INDIVIDUALS**—Know your players. Everyone's brain does not process information in the same manner. Do not assume that you are being totally understood all the time, especially when working with children. If you have players who respond to being yelled at, get them to perform a different way. Yelling seems to be a quick, easy way to coach. This behavior seems to be justified by saying, "My players perform better when I yell and I'm harder on them." I don't know about you, but I do not like to be yelled at any time. I have often in the past been too hard on myself, so I didn't need that reinforced by my coach. Why would anyone think that is a preferred way to coach? If coaches or parents still feel the need to yell, then do it to cheer for your teams. By taking the time to know your players and what really motivates them, you will be able to communicate with them in a much more productive and positive manner.

- **HAVE TEAM MEETINGS**—Meetings that provide a forum for give-and-take with a coach are always a good idea. Air things out. Let your players know what you like about their performance and what you think they can do better. Allow them to do the same. Communication is a two-way street. If all they hear is the coach's dialogue and are not given an opportunity to respond, the coach takes the risk that his players will tune out and shut down.

- BE A GOOD LISTENER—Communication is about more than speaking; it is also about listening. If you expect your players to listen to what you have to say, then you must be willing to listen to them as well.

- THINK BEFORE SPEAKING—Before reacting to a situation, think about the ramifications of what you will say to your team. If your team is not performing, then take a few minutes to figure out what you can say to inspire them to raise their intensity level and fight, rather than discourage them with words that are harsh or demeaning.

- SPEAK WITH RESPECT—Shouting at players or interrupting them when they are speaking is more about the coach than the players.

Most coaches would not allow anyone to do that to them, so why should they act that way with their players?

- EXPLAIN YOURSELF—When discussing game strategies or making adjustments at halftime, explain why you are making changes and what the implications are for them. If players do not understand why you are changing something, they are less likely to be effective in putting those changes into action.

- CREATE AN OPEN DOOR POLICY—Letting players know that you are there for them when they have a problem is essential to your team's success. If they feel they can talk to you—about problems with teammates, team rules, their social life, etc.—you will create an environment that fosters two-way communication and builds trust and respect.

Another form of dialogue that is often overlooked—both in the athletic and business arenas—is body language. A study published in 1988 found that body language accounts for 50 to 75 percent of all communication. Body language includes facial expressions, gestures, and tone of voice. It predates the spoken word and shows how we feel. This is an important form of communication; people pick up on it and get vibes from it. Body language provides a strong form of communication to which few people pay proper attention.

There are a number of ways that your body language can send a message that you do not want to send. For example, if you avoid eye contact, you are giving the message that you lack confidence or are nervous. Slouching also shows a lack of confidence and a lack of authority. Fidgeting may be seen as nervousness or not being prepared. Think of how body language can affect an athlete. A coach can convey a lack of confidence in his players if he does not look them in the eye when he addresses them. Pacing the sideline while a player attempts a crucial free throw may signal a lack of confidence in the player's ability to make the shot. Covering your eyes after a player makes an errant pass or misses a shot sends the message that you are unsure of the player's capabilities. On the other hand, a pat on the back after a miss can tell a player that he still has your confidence. Clapping for a player who has missed several shots tells him to keep plugging away and the shots will fall. These are powerful communication tools, yet not a word has been spoken.

Another effective, yet underused, communication tool is humor. A quick joke can help to defuse difficult situations and relieve tension. I have heard of baseball managers jogging out to the mound for a conference with the pitcher and catcher, with the bases loaded, two outs, and the score tied in the ninth inning. Rather than reminding the pitcher how dire the situation is, the manager tells a joke that loosens the pitcher up so he can get the job done. The manager returns to the dugout, and the relaxed pitcher then strikes out the batter to end the inning.

It is important for coaches to occasionally use humor in challenging situations and to remember that they have to be able to laugh at themselves from time to time. When I was coaching the World TeamTennis Boston Lobsters in 2005, Martina Navratilova was playing on our team. We were playing a home match against Martina Hingis and the New York Sportimes that was being televised on ESPN. Several of my friends, and even people I did not know, told me that they had seen me coaching during that telecast. When "our" Martina was down 3–0 in the singles set against "their" Martina and she came over to me on the sideline and said, "I don't know what to do. What do you think?" Well, all I could think of was: she has won 59 Grand Slam titles and she does not know what to do! I have to admit that I was speechless. So, if Martina Navratilova does not always know what to do on the court, that gives the rest of us hope! How can tennis coaches expect their students to always know what to do?

Humor can also be used as a tool to reprimand without being threatening. By making light of a serious situation, a coach can get his point across without being overly harsh to those whom his humor is directed. The key here is to refrain from using sarcasm as part of your humor; sarcasm is often hurtful and creates further tension. Bev says we need more humor in life, and she is right. If Bev was always serious, I would have quit my comeback a long time ago. You just cannot get that serious about things. Coaches need to remember this and add more humor to their delivery.

In the end, coaches must remember that they are authority figures who are often placed on higher pedestals than parents. They must walk a fine line and demonstrate strength through a caring and empowering manner to teach and inspire their players. Berating and demeaning behavior only builds resentment and destructive anger. For parents, what type of coach do you want working with your children? Your choice will most certainly have lasting effects on those you love.

CHAPTER 5

RESPECT-*PLEASE AND THANK YOU*

It is really quite simple when you think about it: Treat others as you want to be treated. For centuries, diverse cultures around the world have practiced the Golden Rule, a moral tenet endorsed by the world's great religions. *Treat others as you want to be treated.* But this assumes that everyone feels they deserve and want to be treated well. Perhaps this is a big part of why so many people allow others to be disrespectful toward them. A big test is to give someone a compliment and see if they merely say, "Thank you," or if they debate why you were wrong in your thinking. Test yourself when someone says something nice about you. Do you easily accept their kind words?

We see poor sportsmanship on the playing field and broken ethics in the boardroom. Respect has taken a back seat to disrespectful verbal and non-verbal conduct that threatens the very nature of competition. It is time to put respect back into sports, school, business, and life. Twenty years ago, when I was at the top of my game, there were players on the professional tour, both men and women, who behaved poorly. They were rude, they cursed, they argued line calls, and they slammed their racquets at the slightest miss. This still happens today—perhaps even more so. With more television coverage, a much wider audience sees this type of behavior. Players forget that this audience also includes young children. The umpires must quickly diffuse and stop these escalating behaviors by enforcing the rules sooner rather than later. This is not an easy assignment or task. Players who act in this manner must believe their behavior is a necessary component to winning. Can endless screaming, swearing, and racquet abuse be vital to winning? It certainly does not help win the next point.

If I had acted this way on the tennis court when I was growing up, my father would have come out of the stands, onto the court, and defaulted me. I knew that type of behavior was not allowed. In a recent doubles match that I was playing, I was hoping that the umpire would default my partner so the experience would end. Her behavior was so out of control that I did not feel safe. She was slamming her racquet, degrading our opponents, and giving away points because she could not control her emotions. We were in a position to win the match easily until she decided to lose control. She must have felt entitled to act this way. What about me? All I could do was to continue to play my best and hope that she would eventually decide to just play tennis. We did win that match, but it left me very frustrated and, needless to say, I did not have fun. The next day, my partner decided that she was too tired to try in our match. Perhaps if she had kept her feelings in check the night before, she would have been able to give 100 percent in our next match. She showed very little respect for our opponents, the spectators, herself, or me.

I recently watched a match on the USTA tour in which both players were acting horribly. I was so embarrassed. A nice club was hosting the tournament, and several of the club members were watching the match. One player was frequently using the "F" word and the chair umpire was not giving her a warning; I could not imagine why not. If I could hear it from the stands, why couldn't he hear it? Why are players acting this way? Do they think that it will help them win? One of the players gave up 11 points in a row after her tirade. Most of the top players in the game today do not act this way. I am sure they have realized that it not only makes it more difficult to win, it gives away energy and it creates more stress, which can certainly lead to more injuries.

Teaching respect is a critical parental responsibility, yet in today's "me-first" world, respect falls far down on many families' priority list. When I was growing up in Texas, I was taught to address adults as Mr., Mrs., or Ms. as a sign of respect. My parents raised me to be polite and respectful, of both adults and other children. Today, it seems kids are taught that they are equal to adults—that adults have to earn their respect. But it is important for children to be taught that adults are to be listened to and treated with respect. This is a very important role for parents. A dedicated, concerned, and loving parent instills respect, which provides an early discipline that is so important throughout life.

Respect for others and self-respect go hand in hand. It is difficult to feel good about yourself if you act in a disrespectful manner toward others. When you respect others, you feel better about yourself, and this results in more confidence and better performance. Coaches play an essential role in building an athlete's self-respect. Coaches prepare an athlete with techniques and strategies to enhance their skills. They should also teach respect and good sportsmanship, which will serve them well in years to come. The goal is to build the self up rather than tear the self down. How does a coach, especially a parent-coach, help his player, who is losing, when he walks away in the middle of the match? What is the player thinking when he sees his parent/coach leave? To me, this is not a positive show of support or respect for the player. It certainly does not help him want to continue to fight to win.

Showing lack of respect is more of a reflection on the person showing it than it is on the person being disrespected. Many players think the more disruptive they are, the better their chance to impact their opponent to not play well. I see this type of behavior as a weakness that encourages me to fight harder. To me, when players use antics to win, it telegraphs their lack of confidence in their own play. As their opponent, I say, *Bring it on!*

Twenty years ago, tennis players walked on and off the court together, a sign of professional courtesy and respect. Watch Andre Agassi after a match; in victory or defeat, he waits for his opponent so they can walk off the court together. In addition, players today do not show new balls to their opponent, which was another sign of respect. Today, the umpire just says, "New balls in play," so the onus is taken off the player. I do not know if players and coaches are blatantly violating tennis etiquette or if it is ignorance on their part. It would be great to see more emphasis on teaching tennis courtesy to young players by parents, coaches, and officials.

Line calls are another sign of respect in professional tennis. In qualifying matches, there are no umpires, so players must make their own line calls. Many downright blatant bad calls occur in some of these matches. That type of thing happened in junior tennis; it should not happen on the tour. Cheating like that is disrespectful and does not build self respect. Players who cannot win on their own ability may feel that making bad line calls is an acceptable alternative. It is not! And, by the way, it is not acceptable in the juniors either.

Even on tour, where there are umpires, questionable line calls are made. As I have said before, officiating is not an easy task, and no one is perfect. How players deal with this is a sign of respect for the umpire and the opponent, as well as a sign of self-respect. We have all seen tennis players who argue bad calls, scream at the umpire, and throw their racquet. My approach is different: I simply go to the umpire and ask my question: "Are you sure that was out?" I do not swear, scream, throw my racquet, or make a scene. There are ways to question the umpire—or referee, supervisor, teacher, parent—while maintaining respect. There are ways to communicate respectfully without endangering yourself, your opponent, or the fans.

Younger players—and kids—think they need to behave like many of the players they see on television in order to win. Sports are now entertainment. Displays of anger and disrespect frequently ensure that a player makes the highlights on "ESPN Sports Center." Is this what it takes to win? This behavior shows a complete disregard of respect—for the game, for the opponent, and for the player himself.

Respect is the responsibility of everyone involved in sports—players, coaches, parents, officials, and fans. Here are some simple guidelines for demonstrating a healthy respect during athletic competition:

ATHLETES

- Treat everyone with respect.
- Be a good sport, gracious in victory *and* defeat.
- Compliment teammates and opponents on good plays.
- Do not taunt opponents or "trash talk."
- Respect the officials; do not argue calls during or after competition.
- Do not use profane language or make obscene gestures.
- Shake hands with your opponents after the contest.

COACHES

- Respect is expected at all times; develop team rules that require respect for self, opponents, fans, parents, officials, and the game itself.

- Show respect to your players; this will breed respect for themselves and others.

- Never discipline players in a demeaning or embarrassing way.

- Use positive coaching methods to increase self-esteem among players.

- Foster an appreciation for the game.

- Refrain from verbal abuse and demeaning conduct.

- Be a role model; your players will tend to act as you do.

PARENTS

- Conduct yourself appropriately—you are a role model for your child.

- Consider why your child is playing sports—to learn, discover, and refine talents and have fun and prepare for life.

- Teach your child why disrespectful conduct is unacceptable.

- Appreciate good plays by either team.

- Respect the opposing teams' players.

OFFICIALS

- Know the rules and apply them fairly, without favoritism for one team or player.

- Never argue with coaches, players, or fans; if a coach addresses you, speak in a clear, calm tone.

- Remember your role; do not become part of the game.

FANS

- Remember that you are there to support your team, not to demean the opponent.

- Praise athletes for their efforts and show appreciation for outstanding play from either team.

- Do not taunt players, coaches, officials, or the opposing team's fans.

- Respect the judgment and integrity of the officials.

- Do not use obscene language or gestures.

- Participate in supportive cheers with cheerleaders or other fans.

In 1999, 50 influential sports leaders issued the Arizona Sports Summit Accord to "encourage greater emphasis on the ethical and character-building aspects" of athletic competition. This accord is based on the "six pillars of character": trustworthiness, respect, responsibility, fairness, caring, and good citizenship. Today, this accord is the basis for codes of conduct at major colleges, high school athletic associations, youth sports programs, national coaches, and sports official organizations. It has been endorsed by such big-name coaches as Joe Paterno of Penn State, Jim Boeheim of Syracuse University, and U.S. Olympic wrestling coach Dan Gable. This accord can be used to foster an environment of respect in all aspects of athletic competition.

CHAPTER 6

CREATING A TEAM

A team, as defined by the Merriam-Webster dictionary, is a "number of people associated together in work or an activity as a group." Creating a team—and thus teamwork—is the key to success in sports and business as well. Teamwork requires a cooperative effort by everyone involved to reach a common goal, whether that goal is winning the next big game, designing the next great car, or meeting the company's budget projections. Look at the terms we have used thus far in defining team and teamwork: associated together, cooperative effort, common goals. While this is a cliché, it cannot be overstated: There is no "I" in team.

Creating a team is more than just naming players to the roster. It involves goal setting, risk taking, cooperation, leadership, creativity, decision making, communication, dialogue, respect, motivation, flexibility, and trust. Building an effective team is not easy, and keeping it together is quite a challenge. It is, however, essential for success.

Our culture is fascinated by individual accomplishments, especially in "team" sports. We hear on TV and read in newspapers about how many home runs Barry Bonds has hit, and how many points Shaquille O'Neil scored last night. Many players have outstanding individual statistics, yet their teams have never won a championship. Home-run king Barry Bonds has never been on a World Series-winning team. Until recently, Jerome Bettis, one of the all-time leading rushers in the NFL, had never won a Super Bowl. Nevertheless, their individual accomplishments are impressive.

Barry Bonds has often been viewed as not being a good teammate and has had difficulty with the San Francisco fans. Controversy seems to follow him. Whether this perception is true or not, something in his actions must have fostered this. Jerome Bettis is beloved by both his teammates and the Pittsburgh Steelers' fans. Bettis' demeanor and constant positive energy have helped his team to accomplish the near impossible—a wild card team on the road beating all the top-rated teams to advance to the 2006 Super Bowl. His teammates are motivated to win for him. That is the ultimate compliment from your team. His dream to end his incredible career in Detroit with a Super Bowl ring has now been fulfilled. Nice guys DO finish first! Which player do you wish your child to emulate?

To understand the essence of team, look back to 1972 when the Dallas Cowboys, then known as "America's Team," capped a great season by winning Super Bowl VI over the Miami Dolphins. Led by their MVP quarterback Roger Staubach, the Cowboys worked as an effective unit—a team—to shut down the tough Miami offense and defense. It was the first time in Super Bowl history that a team did not score a touchdown. This Dallas team had its share of stars—future Hall of Famers Staubach, Bob Lilly, Lance Alworth, and Mike Ditka among them— but these players all put their egos aside for the team's benefit, and they won.

Some sports do not lend themselves to what we traditionally consider a team, tennis and golf among them. But the golfer and tennis player are not alone; they are not islands unto themselves. Coaches, trainers, and physical therapists all work with these individual athletes to create a team environment in order to win. The same rules apply: cooperation, communication, trust, and goal setting. In many ways, teamwork is even more essential for such a small group. If a tennis player has only four people on his "team," one person who is not doing his job can wreak more havoc than one player out of 50-some in the NFL who goes his own way.

So then, how does one create a team? The elements that I mentioned earlier are the building blocks of a team—whether it is a professional sports team, a small business team, or a work team in a large corporation. Let's talk about some of these in more detail.

COMMUNICATION

Effective communication is vital for the development of a good team. Clear, positive communication—coach to coach, coach to athlete, athlete to athlete, coach to parent (this is huge in youth sports)—allows a team to operate more smoothly. Through effective communication, teams can develop and understand goals and work toward them. Players can air their concerns about the team, as well as their own development. Even though the goal is to perform as a single unit, it is important to recognize each individual's wants and needs and to allow players to communicate those wants and needs among their teammates and with their coaches. Open lines of communication also enable teams to consider new ideas and suggestions. A team is a group-learning experience, and everyone on the team has something to offer. Encourage everyone to share their ideas with the coaching staff—you never know what you will find. A team that communicates well relies on feedback, both good and bad. An environment that stifles communication does not allow for the give-and-take of constructive dialogue. The ability to learn from this constructive dialogue is a positive, healthy way for a team to improve.

ATTITUDE AND EGO

Team attitude and team ego go hand-in-hand and are crucial for team building. A good team attitude can be defined by how well each athlete accepts his role on the team and performs that role for the team's benefit. Coaches can help create a positive team attitude by setting a worthy example, accepting all the responsibilities of their position and not just the ones they enjoy. By doing this, players will begin to understand how individuals performing their roles to the best of their ability can create a successful team.

We have all heard or read about team "chemistry," or how well players blend together and get along. This chemistry helps to build teams both physically and emotionally. It allows underdogs to overcome the odds to win games that, on paper, they have no business winning. This chemistry is the essence of team attitude, and it applies in both athletic and business settings. Coaches can build chemistry through frequent positive feedback, open lines of communication, asking for input from players, team meetings, and by reminding each player how valuable they are to the team. A team with good chemistry becomes more confident, trusting that each player will perform his role and put his team in a position to succeed.

A byproduct of team attitude is team ego. This is the "we-instead-of-me" attitude that puts the team first. Players must set aside their own ego for the good of the team. Team ego is about pride in yourself, your teammates, and your team or organization. Individual success is important and should be recognized, however the team comes first.

MOTIVATION

Regardless of the team's level—youth, high school, college, or the pros—players must be motivated to be successful, even winning teams. Teams that are not motivated are flat and, unless they completely overpower their opponent, they are unlikely to succeed. Motivation means finding a reason to perform to the best of your ability in order to achieve team goals. This is a joint endeavor between coaches and players. The coach and his players are responsible for being mentally and physically prepared to play and to put the team in a position to win. This is not just the coach's responsibility. The players must be self motivated also. Self motivation is one of the biggest contributors to success. One cannot always rely on teammates or coaches or parents for motivation. You have to want it yourself, otherwise you will not persevere when a difficult challenge presents itself. Motivate yourself to help the team achieve its goals.

There are a number of ways to motivate athletes. Goal setting is an important one, giving players something meaningful to strive for. These goals, however, must be realistic. Teams with a realistic set of goals are more likely to succeed than those for whom expectations are too high. Goals should be both short-term and long-term. Short-term goals are measurable steps on the way to achieving longer-term objectives and providing players a sense of achievement along the way.

Positive reinforcement is another motivational tool. Speaking directly with players about their performance can help set standards that can motivate them. While many coaches rely on constructive criticism, complimenting good effort and performance are much more effective techniques for motivating athletes. It is important to praise the team, as well as the individual.

Athletes are more likely to perform well for coaches who listen to their suggestions and comments. Many coaches believe they are the final word—the word of God—and rarely, if ever, listen to the players on their teams. I tell the young players that I coach, that it is my responsibility to demonstrate to them that what I am saying to them and asking them to do works. It is up to me to find a way to connect with all of my players. When players have a voice, they become more motivated to perform at their peak for the team's benefit.

Vince Lombardi was a good strategist and a master motivator. He realized what motivated each individual on his team. What worked with Paul Hornung did not necessarily work for others. He found the right "cues" to get Hornung to play his best. He took a quieter approach with other players, offering positive reinforcement in an effort to get them to perform. Coaches must discover what cues work best for each player and then use them accordingly.

TEAM RULES

Team rules can help hold teams together. Teams function best when rules are obeyed, and everyone acts as one unit. Rules are as important as performance, but they must be applied fairly and consistently across the board. No one player—regardless of his ability in the sport—is above his teammates when it comes to rules and discipline. Too many rules, however, can have a negative impact on a team, as can frivolous ones. Rules must be consistent with team goals and, even more importantly, they must be enforced.

One key to rule setting is team participation in developing the rules. If rules are simply edicts from the coach, then players do not have any ownership and are more likely to disregard them. However, if they have participated in developing the team's rules, they are given part ownership of them and have a responsibility to see that they are followed.

Team responsibility goes hand-in-hand with these rules. This stresses that good behavior is the *team's* responsibility. When the whole team has to run extra sprints because of the negative behavior of one teammate, you can be sure that teammate's behavior will change pretty quickly.

Another key to team participation is self-discipline—what you do when no one is looking. This includes how you prepare for practice and games, the standards which you maintain for yourself off the field of play, and how you conduct yourself as an individual before, during, and after competition. A player with self-discipline is one who understands that he represents himself, his family, his team, and his community.

ROLE OF CAPTAIN

A very important role on the team is that of team captain. The obvious leader of a team is the head coach, but leadership is also everyone's responsibility. A leader does not have to necessarily be the player with the most talent, but the one other players look up to and respect. In many cases, these players are named team captain. Being named a team captain is a big honor and comes with the responsibility of motivating others, resolving conflicts, educating younger players, integrating new players, and communicating concerns to the coaching staff. An effective captain shows commitment to the team and a good attitude—in short, leadership.

Superior athletic ability is not a prerequisite to being a captain, yet Penn State researchers have found that when NHL players take the post as team captain, they play better than they did in the years they didn't have this leadership responsibility. In essence, they found that these players realized how important their role was on the team and took their game to a higher level, providing the leadership that is so essential. Many team captains show their leadership in ways other than on-field accomplishment. Some help struggling teammates, others view their role as cheerleaders to help build team cohesion.

It is important to remember, however, that while a team captain is the first among equals, he is not above the team or its rules or its goals. He is a member of the team like everyone else, but has been given certain responsibilities based on the trust and respect of his teammates. He must still obey the rules, he must still practice hard, and he must still work toward the team's goals.

Helen Keller, for whom the concept of team had a far greater meaning than any athletic endeavor, once said, "Alone we can do so little; together we can do so much." While she probably did not realize it at the time, she was defining what a team is all about.

CHAPTER 7

MANAGING YOUR MIND

It has been said that sports are 95 percent inspiration and 5 percent perspiration. Many athletes, especially at elite levels, have similar physical attributes and skills, and more time is spent training the body for the demands and challenges of sports. However, it is the mind that controls the body. Few athletes—or coaches—spend time training the mind for athletic competition.

The following is a good example of how even a world class athlete had not even considered the power the mind has over one's performance. The night before the 2005 World TeamTennis semifinals in Sacramento, California, I had dinner with Martina Navratilova, Bev, and my friend Marc Gearin. Marc asked Martina what she thought separated the top tennis players from the others on the professional tour since they all have great strokes and are good athletes. He also wondered if there was another Martina Navratilova developing among the players. Martina responded that a combination of athleticism, training, and talent makes the difference among players. She also felt there could certainly be other players who could develop and perhaps be as successful as she had been.

At that point, Bev turned to Martina and said, "So you think there are players who have your mind? How many others have your mental toughness and play the way you have played the game for so long? There is only one Martina Navratilova." She listened and said she had not thought of it in that way. Of course, she then agreed with what Bev had said. Most people do look at sport from the physical side. Even Martina forgot that NO ONE has her mind!

The greatest challenge in sports is the mental one. Athletes need proper self-motivation and a mental edge to win. The athlete's state of mind directly affects his performance and the eventual outcome of the game. The top athletes in the world tend to deliver their best performances when they are physically relaxed and mentally focused. When athletes fail, the first thing to go is often their mental edge. That is, they are more physically fit than they are mentally fit.

In a study conducted by Loyola Marymount University, 658 coaches and young athletes were asked to choose five out of 128 characteristics that they believed would make a winning athlete. Half of the characteristics they chose were physical ones, the other half were psychological ones. Most of the coaches chose characteristics like "loves to play," "positive attitude," "coachable," "self-motivated," and "strives to improve." They also identified constant criticism and negative feedback as among the most damaging factors for young athletes. All of these are governed by or affect the athlete's mind and, ultimately, his body. A number of things can influence an athlete's state of mind: the pressure and desire to win, past success or failure in competition, adversity, stress, and high expectations (of parents, coaches, and the athlete himself).

The mind controls what is going to happen. Too often, an athlete's mind is filled with negative thoughts, self-doubt, and harmful self-dialogue about his talent and skill. When the mind concentrates on these things, it leads to failure since the athlete focuses too much on what he is doing wrong—and criticizing himself for it—rather than focusing on the positive aspects of his play. My mental mindset is one reason I have been able to successfully come back on the tour after 14 years. I now realize that focusing on my misses causes me to miss even more.

Please note that I am purposely not using the word "mistake." This word is very powerful and leaves too much of a negative imprint on a player's mind. So I focus on what I am doing well, understanding that I will miss some shots when I am playing each point at my best intensity level. When I gave more attention to a missed shot than to a well-executed one, I often gave away too many "free points" after the miss. But my "bring on the next point" attitude punishes my opponent, not me. This has helped me get better faster.

Changing your self-talk takes practice. The first thing you need to be aware of is what you are saying to yourself. Once you become mindful of all the negative things that you are saying to yourself, you can then do something about it. The best thing is to replace negative dialogue with positive dialogue. Rather than saying, *You idiot. I can't believe you missed that shot again,* you might say, *No problem. I'll make it the next time.* Your internal dialogue will either enhance your play or undermine your play. Do you want to use words that empower or words that deflate? The choice is yours.

An athlete's mind is fragile and delicate; it should be handled with care. Most athletes are well prepared physically, but their mind is what will make or break them. They have to be aware of their inner dialogue and how this affects their mindset during competition. Some of today's best athletes have screaming dialogues with themselves, saying, *I'm terrible. Why do I even play?* or even worse. One cannot win or even enjoy the contest when he talks like this. When I play someone who acts like this, I just wait until that type of behavior starts and then let the player beat herself. They know this happens, yet they will not change their behavior. One player told me, "I just get so angry, I can't control myself."

Anger is one of the most destructive emotions. It can come out in several ways. When I was younger, my anger would be demonstrated at times by my giving less than my best effort in matches. The player referenced above was showing her anger by being physically destructive and saying hurtful things. When I played on the tour in the early '80s, I was good at keeping my anger inside. I very rarely acted out on the tennis court. But it still took my energy to keep anger from getting the best of me. Believe me, I got angry at myself, I just did not show it very often on the court. I knew myself well enough and had learned through experience that when I allowed my anger to get out of control, there was no way I was going to win.

Anger is a habit, so you need to break the habit of responding to certain situations with anger. The only way to accomplish this is first with awareness, and then with practice. First, you must become aware and admit that your anger is causing problems in your tennis matches, your life, your personal relationships, or your career. Then you must realize the physical responses associated with your anger. What are the physical warning signs? Do your muscles start tensing? Does your stomach start churning? When you realize your physical warning signs, you must talk to yourself, calm yourself down, take a walk, count to ten, slow down your breathing— whatever works. You must stop letting your anger control you. Then you must avoid getting angry. You must replace the anger response with something else. What will you choose to do the next time you practice or play a match? Will you choose emotions and actions that will help you to win, or will you choose emotions and actions that will cause you to lose?

Regardless of the situation—be it sports, business, or relationships—our mind has a choice. We can be reactive or proactive. Which one will create a winning situation? The mind has to make choices all the time. In tennis, the mind has about 3 seconds to choose and execute; in baseball, the batter has even less time. Employees have seconds to defuse or exacerbate certain situations. The choices belong to each of us. If we are usually negative, we will make choices that create even more problems. If we are positive and responsible, we will make choices that enhance both ourselves and others as well. If more athletes today would practice empowering their minds as well as their techniques, it would be much easier for them to win.

In my recent comeback in professional tennis, my philosophy has been to believe that things happen for a reason. Whenever something happens that is not the result I wanted, I accept it, put it behind me, and move on. I do not dwell on the loss. I have created a mindset that allows me to just play, improve, and enjoy the points and the crowd without dwelling on what did not happen.

It was not always that way. At the very beginning of my career, I played in a warm-up grass court tournament just before Wimbledon. On match point against a player ranked in the top 5 in the world, she hit a shot over the baseline that was clearly out and called out by the linesperson. I had won, and was about to shake her hand at the net when the umpire overruled the linesperson and called the ball good. Can you imagine an umpire waiting until we both came to the net to change the call? The umpire overruling at that moment was hard for me to swallow. I completely fell apart, losing the third set badly. A win would have been huge for me at that point in my career. My career could have taken a completely different path. After the match, I was depressed for quite a long time. The whole experience had a negative impact on me, costing me matches and tournaments because of my state of mind.

If that same scenario were to play out today, I would handle myself much differently because of my belief that everything happens for a reason. I would be angry and disappointed, but I would not view it as the end of the world. Rather, I would treat it as just one more match and accept that my loss was meant to be, as I could not control the umpire's decision. I would use that experience to become tougher and not succumb to the failure of that particular moment. I would tell myself that, in reality, there are many more matches to be played. If only back then I had thought that training my mind was just as important as practicing my game....

One of my doubles partners lost her serve during a recent match we played. It affected her for the rest of the match. Rather than forget about it and play stronger, she dwelled on the fact that she had lost her serve. All this did was give our opponents many free points simply because of the way she felt. Behaving like this was not only a waste of time it made me wonder if she was really able to accept winning. Sadly, she continued to lose her serve.

In my comeback, I have tried to act as if nothing bothers me, win or lose. It is all in how

I carry myself and how I speak. I do not act discouraged—even if I am. I am just tricking my mind. Your mind can bring you down before your body does. Watch Roger Federer. He ignores his misses. By the time he is off the court, he is over whatever negative things happened in his match. He plays at his best intensity, win or lose. Even when his ankle was sprained, he continued to fight and almost won his match in the season-ending ATP Tennis Master Cup in Shangai against David Nalbandian. He, too, was tricking his mind.

Pittsburgh Steelers' coach Bill Cowher recently told his team at halftime to pretend that they were starting the first quarter so they would continue to look and play strong. They did just that and went on to win Super Bowl XL. In chapter 8, I will talk more about perception and the role it plays in creating a winning attitude.

One thing to remember is that athletes need to practice managing their thoughts and behavior, as well as what they choose to say during competition. There are only three things we can truly control: what we think, what we say, and how we act. We can either partake in poor behavior, or not. We can say negative things, or not. We can react negatively to things, or we can handle them appropriately. Athletes who are able to handle their emotions, manage their misses, and control their nerves are the ones who will be more successful. All athletes are involved in self-dialogue; the ones who engage in positive dialogue are the ones who succeed. This takes awareness and practice. Can you imagine that most of us have to practice being kind and compassionate to ourselves? You would think that would be easy. It would certainly allow winning to occur more easily and more quickly.

Observe some top athletes and you will see this in action. Donovan McNabb and Tom Brady are both very good quarterbacks, but their mental toughness seems to be quite different. Their 2005 Super Bowl performances are a good illustration. Under pressure toward the end of the game, McNabb appeared to lower his intensity with his passes and could not mentally or physically pull out a victory. Brady, on the other hand, is not the natural athlete that McNabb is, yet his mind is so finely tuned that he gets the job done when the pressure is on. As in other Super Bowls and important games, he calmly led the Patriots to victory because his mind was able to rule his body and set the tone for success. The minds of these two great quarterbacks handled these crucial moments quite differently.

Managing the mind is not an occasional thing for an athlete; it must be practiced constantly. Consider the number of sports psychologists who are now being used by teams from high school through professional levels to create a positive, winning mindset among athletes. These professionals help athletes prepare for competition and maintain positive thinking in the heat of the contest.

One of the most important times for an athlete to manage his mind is well before the game or match even begins. There are a number of ways that this can be done. Ivan Lendl would pretend that he had already lost the match and then would just go and play. I play tricks on my mind, saying to myself, *I don't care if I win or lose; I just want to do the best I can.* That takes some of the pressure off of winning. Of course I *do* care if I win or lose, but if that is the main focus, it will make me so tight that I will not be able to perform to the best of my ability. I have learned that I play best when I focus on one point at a time rather than thinking about winning or losing. I manage my intensity level on my shots so that I do not waste energy.

Athletes need to find their best intensity level in order to be successful. This will reduces stress and tension and allow for better performance. (I talk more about intensity level in Chapter 11)

Some athletes manage their mind by goal setting. They know what they want to achieve and what they must do in order to win. They also realize what distracts them. Goal setting helps many athletes to achieve more and to perform better, and also helps build self-confidence and motivation to continue improving. Realistic goal setting can enable athletes to perform at a higher level. But being the best on a team does not ensure that things will always go perfectly in competition. In fact, expecting perfection can backfire and, ultimately, cause disappointment. I mentioned in the introduction that my perfectionism had caused me to feel as if I were fighting myself instead of my opponent. This took away my joy from playing tennis, even when I won.

When I played on the tour in the '80s, I had, perhaps, only a couple of matches a year when I felt as if I were hitting the ball perfectly. Many players become quite frustrated when they feel they are not hitting the ball well. It is about how you respond during those times that your timing is not "perfect" that will define you. It is easier to win and be positive when everything feels great, of course. The real challenge is to not judge your performance and win during those times when things just do not feel "right." Again, the mind has a choice during every moment of competition. I now choose to have reactions and thoughts that maximize my performance to help me win. I know you would choose these thoughts, too!

Some athletes use visualization (including myself at one point in my career) in which they simulate in their mind the game or match they are about to play. By using this technique, they see themselves performing perfectly. In particular, I remember one match I was playing in Oklahoma City. During one of the changeovers, I visualized myself holding my serve. After the changeover, I went to receive serve. Well, it *was* my serve. That is how powerful the mind is. I had already won my serve in my mind during the changeover!

Coaches play a key role in a player's mental preparation. Like many athletes, however, coaches do not spend much time on the mental aspects of competition. They need to understand that the mind is just as important to a player's development as their physical skills. They should put more emphasis on this part of player preparation.

In addition, coaches need to provide their players with the best tools available to prepare for competition. What the coach decides to dwell on—positive or negative—is very important. By keeping the atmosphere positive and enjoyable, coaches can help players create a balance between hard work and fun. They can emphasize the positive aspects of a player's or a team's performance and reward those efforts. Rather than a big pre-game pep talk, coaches should focus on specific goals and strategies for the contest. A roaring pep talk will not prepare them to play if they are not ready to do so on their own. However, positive comments from coaches can help to create a winning mindset and attitude among individual players and the team as a whole. Negative comments, on the other hand, can make or break a player mentally.

When you are watching an athletic event on television, how many outcomes are determined by small defining moments when athletes must make the best choice and execute? At these times, athletes must not only have the mindset that allows them to win, they must also be able to accept the joy and happiness of what they achieve. It sounds simple, but it is not if a player is constantly being bombarded with negative talk. How can a coach be certain that a player will perform well in the crucial moments instead of creating circumstances that lead to more negative outcomes? As I have become more comfortable with accolades, I have seen both my tennis performance and my life become easier.

Parents can also help their children maintain a mental edge in sports by controlling their own emotions and handling themselves appropriately during games. When kids see their parents act irresponsibly at games, that behavior affects them also (see chapter 9 on being a role model). Parents need to reinforce the positive aspects of their child's sports experience: to participate, have fun, and learn important life lessons. By patiently listening to your child after a loss or an "off" performance you can help your child to develop a mindset to learn from losses and use those experiences to become better and develop a winning attitude. Why would any loving, responsible parent want their child to think that motivation depends upon criticism and negative self-talk? By focusing on the positive things, a true, winning outcome can be achieved. Children will gain more confidence and independence, and be proud of themselves and their accomplishments.

In managing their minds, athletes must understand how a negative mindset affects their performance. They must give less attention to their misses and give much more credence to hitting a good shot or playing a good point. With everything else being equal, the athlete with the mental edge will, more often than not, win. How a player chooses to see a situation, to manage his nerves and emotions and talk to himself after misses, are key ingredients in creating a winning mindset. If every athlete could find a mental weapon, often more important than a physical one, he would allow himself to win with much less self-imposed stress and effort.

CHAPTER 8

IT'S ALL ABOUT PERCEPTION

Many sports teams have learned that the victor is not always the one with the superior skills. How many times has an underdog overcome a superior opponent to win a game? Is this luck? Maybe. Is it better mental preparation? Perhaps. Or is it how the opponent perceives the underdog and how the underdog perceives itself? Many times, it's all about perception.

My friend who coaches Pop Warner football tells a story of how perception can be used as a tool for winning. Two teams line up for the mandatory pre-game weigh-in. One team, looking to be a bit bigger and tougher, lines up with their shirts untucked and generally disheveled and disorganized. His team, wary of their opponent to begin with, looks like a team: jerseys tucked in, a straight, single-file line of players preparing themselves for the contest. Who wins? Not the bigger, tougher team with the better record, but the underdog. Why? It could be that the team that really looked like a team was perceived by their opponent to be better prepared and more willing to do what was necessary to win. Or perhaps my friend's team simply perceived themselves to be better because of the way they looked and conducted themselves prior to the game. This gave them the confidence to overcome a physically superior team. They owned the field before they ran out to play.

I have learned that in sports, business, and life, how you present yourself can prepare you to win. How you carry yourself and behave on the court can be just as important to winning as how well you serve and volley. How you respond to adversity in the boardroom —in a calm, controlled manner or with anger and disrespect—can be a key to winning in business as well. It is not always about your game skills but about the things that you can control—your behavior and what and how you say things on the court, on the field, or in the boardroom.

Perception frequently differs from reality! In my former position as Director of the

Learning Center for Dean College in Franklin, Massachusetts, I understood that employees depended on me not only for their jobs but for their work environment. I always made an effort to smile and be engaging. Walking deep in thought with my head down might have been perceived by my employees that something was wrong. My behavior was important to ensure a more relaxed and productive work atmosphere. I was mindful of how I would be perceived every moment of the work day. Many managers seem to create the opposite atmosphere, thinking it would increase productivity and profit.

Even if you cannot win based on the skills you have, your demeanor and body language can make your opponent wonder. If your opponent sees you slouch while awaiting serve or shuffling with your head down after a lost point, it may signal a weakness in your game that can be exploited. But if you move around the court with meaning and look firmly at your opponent as she serves, it will show confidence despite the score or your skill level. The choice is yours to make.

During my comeback in professional tennis, I have been able to win matches, not through overpowering physical skills, but with my on-court demeanor. Even when I am discouraged with my play, I carry myself in a way that does not display how I might truly feel. Rather, I conduct myself in a manner which says, *Yeah, I missed that shot, but I'll get the next one and win.* Nothing my opponent does can deter me. If I miss, I will make my opponent pay for it, not make myself pay for the miss. I just consider it a fluke and move on. That perception of confidence can be disarming to an opponent—though I may not feel confident about my game on the inside. I have coached my mind to believe that I can win. This is the first step toward winning.

If winning is the goal, you must coach your mind to win (more about this in Chapter 11). When opponents see a weakness in you—in what you say or how you behave—they will exploit it. Why is it that the mental part of the game is considered to be so important, yet very few players take the time to train their mind at the same time they are learning the physical skills of the game? Without this training they are unable to coordinate the physical and mental skills for a successful outcome.

Sometimes one must take reality and create a different perception. Bev tells me to "fake it" when I am not confident in my play on the court. This has been necessary when I have not had ample time to train. If my mind is clouded with doubt and confusion, why exhibit that to my opponent? She will just take advantage of those moments of weakness and defeat me. So I fake it; I pretend that I am confident in my game so that my opponent will perceive that confidence. If I fake it well enough, I may even be able to trick my own mind into believing that I am playing well. Then I can use that to exploit my opponent's flaws. How we perceive ourselves is just as important as how others perceive us. If one feeds the mind negative comments, these emerge on the court or in a business meeting as well. Self-talk can be sabotaging if not done in a positive manner.

Recently, one of my doubles partners was playing a singles match in a tournament in Georgia. She did not feel well prepared for the match and had the choice of either talking herself into being prepared to play or torturing herself with negative self-talk. Unfortunately, she chose to torture herself, saying throughout the match, *I don't belong here. I haven't trained hard enough so I don't deserve to win.* She was down 4–1 in the third set and battled back to 4–all, eventually losing the match 6–4 despite having a strong chance to win. Why did she lose? She chose "self-talk" that helped give away crucial games and ultimately the match to her opponent. She also created more stress for herself, which could have increased her risk for injury, a worse outcome than losing. She could have reversed her negative feelings by talking to herself in a more positive manner. Why would she choose to punish herself and not permit herself to win? All she had to do was fake it—pretend that she was prepared to play and win, rather than permit her negative feelings to lead to a loss.

Another player I know was once top-40 in the world in women's singles, yet she perceived herself quite differently. Following major knee surgery, she chose to train by running sprints on a hard-surface court. She was not confident enough in her skills to pull herself through. This was self-sabotage, self-torture. She perceived herself to be less of a player than she actually was. She felt she had to put herself through this overly rigorous training program in order to regain her game after the injury, but this only served to prolong the pain in her recovery.

Maximizing performance is essential to success. How do you react when things do not go your way? When champions miss, they take it as an opportunity, not as a giveaway. Many players become angry when things go awry. This is an opportunity for your opponent to exploit. When you are angry, you cannot be calm. It is a calm, focused mind that helps you play your best. If you can learn to ignore adversity and say to yourself, "Next point," your concentration and intensity level will not be interrupted. A competitor does not like to see his opponent exhibit strong body language throughout a match. It is very unnerving, to say the least. Think of how many "free points" one can get by not showing the opponent how you feel. My opponent will never know that I am angry. Recently, I witnessed a world-class tennis player become so angry that she lost 11 straight points. After that, she chose to control her anger, and she almost won the match. If only she had done that from the beginning, she most likely would have won the match.

One cannot play a sport (or succeed in a business setting) without some emotion. It is much easier to have positive emotions when things are going well. When one is presented with difficult situations, it is very important to remain calm so that your mind can make wise choices. If you are angry within or give it outward evidence, that emotion does not help you to win, whether in sports competition, business, or personal relationships. Once more, we all have the power to choose our reactions every moment of each day. What emotions and reactions will *you* choose in order to be a better coach, player, parent, boss, or friend?

CHAPTER 9

YOU'RE A ROLE MODEL

Like most youngsters, I had good role models when I was growing up—my parents, coaches, and teachers, people who had a positive influence on my life and my development as a tennis player and as a person. As a professional athlete, I, too, am someone's role model. Whatever your position in life—parent, teacher, coach, clergy, police officer—you're a role model also.

A role model's job is easily defined: act appropriately and treat people, especially young people, with respect. If you are a kind, considerate person, you want to be a role model. If you really care about people, you want to be a role model. If you want to inspire others to do better, you want to be a role model.

Having a good role model helps children focus on their goals and achieve success. In fact, studies have shown that children who have a good role model are more likely to reach their goals. Almost all successful people have had role models. Bill Clinton's role model was John F. Kennedy, and Henry Ford's was Thomas Edison, for instance. Role models open the mind to possibilities that may seem out of reach. Without role models, children could never dare to dream big.

The sports world is an ideal place to find a role model, good and bad. Sports are so highly visible and publicized that athletes must consider themselves as role models. Whether they admit it, like it, or want to be one, athletes, especially professional athletes, *are* role models. Athletes at higher collegiate levels and on Olympic teams often serve as role models to children as well. An Olympic decathlete remarked about being a positive influence in children's lives: "We want to be role models. We want to be good examples of what athletes are supposed to be like. We want kids to look up to us. It's something we've been dreaming about since we were kids."

One of my role models in professional sports was Billie Jean King. She was also my favorite doubles partner. Not only was she a top player, but she was kind and supportive, and has done so much for women's sports. I am happy that she thought I did the same for her AND that I made her laugh. Martina Navratilova falls into this category as well. She is one of the greatest athletes of all time; she is also intelligent, inspiring, kind to others, and has had the courage to live her life her way. Billie Jean and Martina are great role models.

Tom Brady may be the quintessential role model. He is a great athlete who has won Super Bowls and Super Bowl MVP awards. Brady goes out of his way to be a good guy. He is the ultimate teammate, putting team ahead of self, and is one of the top choices when other NFL players are asked who they would most like to have on their team. He wins with dignity, pride, and humility, yet the size of his head has not changed with all this success. He is a genuine positive role model.

Among today's tennis players, Kim Clijsters and Roger Federer are not only top players, but top role models as well. They are also among the players' favorites. They show that you can be #1 in the world without antics, showboating, rudeness, or disrespect. Their enjoyment of the game is inspiring; thus they are good role models.

Bev had the opportunity to meet and play tennis with Robert Plant, the former lead singer for the rock band Led Zeppelin, who now has a very successful solo career. Bev mentioned that he was such a nice guy and that the fans just adored him. He told her: "I could be a real jerk and still have all this adulation. I choose to be a nice guy. Why not?"

While there are many positive role models in sports, there are also a lot of negative role models—and we can spot them from a mile away. They get all the attention with their antics and boorish behavior. Hundreds of professional athletes, and countless amateurs as well, perform community service at hospitals, schools, boys-and-girls clubs, and community centers, yet this does not often get headlines. Taking out a Sharpie to sign a football after scoring a touchdown gets on the highlight reel. So does the ever-so-slow home run trot, the dance after sacking the quarterback, and smashing a tennis racquet after a miss. Are these really the people we want our kids to look up to? I do not think so.

We hear on the sports report and read in the newspaper about athletes who get arrested for drug and alcohol abuse or are suspended for taking performance-enhancing substances. Some of these are middle-of-the-road athletes who do not otherwise make the sports pages, but a good number are successful sports figures. Are these the ones we want our children to emulate?

A parent is a role model whether he wants to be or not. Everyone is a role model for someone, many times for someone they do not even know! There is a saying that the only way to raise a decent human being is to be one yourself. This is so true. Parents who regularly criticize their children or act disrespectfully toward others are teaching their children to do the same. If parents want their children to respect others' rights and feelings, they must respect their own children's rights and feelings. When a parent teaches a child to behave one way and then he does the opposite, the child will become confused and wonder which is the right way to behave—and often will behave similarly to their parents. We have all seen out-of-control parents at youth sporting events yelling at coaches, jawing with the officials, and berating their children. These are role models also. They are examples of how not to behave. Children who see this behavior in their parents are more likely to act that way themselves.

Coaches also have an important obligation to be a good role model to the players on their teams, and most coaches do this admirably. Among their responsibilities are teaching game skills, setting high moral standards, being positive, and teaching fairness and sportsmanship. Coaches are sometimes the only positive role model in their players' lives. Their words and actions leave a lasting impression. Coaches should carefully consider what they say and do, and how they say it and do it. Many of us look back on our youth coaches and model our behavior on their examples. That is the ultimate byproduct of being a role model.

A good way to determine if your behavior is worthy of role-model status is to actually videotape yourself for two weeks, or at least pretend that you have done so. Does your behavior change because the camera is recording it? Is your conduct—what you say and what you do—acceptable for the audience for which it is intended? Do you treat people with the respect and dignity they deserve? Do you have what it takes to be a positive role model?

CHAPTER 10

ATTITUDE IS EVERYTHING

Attitude is defined as behavior that indicates thoughts, feelings, and opinions. Thus, a positive attitude is one that displays *positive* thoughts, feelings, and opinions. Attitude is a mindset that becomes what life is all about. Attitude is how you react to situations and decide what to do in that moment. Attitude is everything—in sports, business, and life.

My recent comeback is a good example of how attitude can affect performance. At the beginning, I thought I could go in and win some matches right away. Instead, I was losing badly in singles, and doubles was not much better. I became very discouraged and my attitude suffered. I was focusing on winning or losing and creating expectations that were way too high. Needless to say, this did not help me to play better tennis. I decided that I must focus on one point at a time, rather than on winning or losing; I must seem confident whether I felt confident or not, and remember that the spectators enjoyed watching me perform whether I won or lost. This change in attitude helped me to move ahead in my comeback and become more comfortable on the tennis court. It also helped me to start winning more matches. The lesson: change your attitude first and good results will follow.

Some of my opponents are quite negative about themselves. This is seen in their body language and how they carry themselves. You can hear it in what they say to themselves and to others. This attitude is not helping them perform well.

Having a positive attitude is a simple, easy thing to do, yet it is something that people rarely think about. Look at Andre Agassi and Roger Federer, arguably two of the world's best tennis players. They have such positive attitudes. They have a very different language than everyone else and just love to play the game. That is why they're where they are and why they have won so often. They follow a very simple creed: Attitude first, then results.

Professional sports, however, are filled with examples of negative attitudes. For instance, consider Terrell Owens. He is one of the most talented receivers in football, perhaps in the history of the game. And yet, not too many players have wanted him as a teammate because of his attitude. T.O.'s remarkable performance in the 2004 Super Bowl was overshadowed by his attitude and behavior. If he could be more of a team player and leader, he would certainly help his teammates achieve their maximum potential. He has the mental and the physical skills to be the best wide receiver in the game, but he must share these skills and help his team. Apparently T.O. now agrees. Since joining the Dallas Cowboys, T.O. has said, *I want to be a good teammate. I try to take the leadership role and encourage our younger guys and help them develop their game.* As a life long Dallas Cowboy's fan, I am looking forward to watching the new T.O., dynamic and exciting as a player; a great teammate and leader as a man. The complete athlete.

The New England Patriots exemplify what having a positive attitude is all about. Their attitude is "team first." It is all about the team and winning championships. With the Pats, attitude is everything—and all they have to show for it are three Super Bowl wins in four years! The San Antonio Spurs in the NBA are the same way. Coach Greg Popovich specifically drafts players who are good role models and have high principles and standards. This philosophy has engendered a good attitude among his players and has propelled them to the top. Tim Duncan is one of the best players in the NBA today, yet rarely, if ever, do you hear him spout off about himself. He is a quiet professional, with a positive attitude, who is a winner.

At the professional level, there is sometimes very little a coach can do to change a negative attitude. That should have been addressed much earlier! They are adults, and the goal in professional sports is to win. Many coaches weigh the risks and benefits of attitude versus physical skill. The coach needs the most talented players to win, so attitude often takes a back seat to physical ability. In youth sports, high school, and even collegiate athletics, coaches can have an immeasurable impact on their players' attitudes. Coaches should be positive role models who teach their charges to compete, be good sports, and have fun at the same time. This rubs off on kids.

It is easy to tell those who have a good attitude or a bad attitude by watching players practice and play in games. Those with positive attitudes see the game as just that—a game, with the opportunity to learn a skill, compete, grow, increase their confidence and, most importantly, have fun. Those with bad attitudes see the game as a pressure-filled competition. They are often the ones who complain a lot, whine about the officiating, and make excuses for their misses. It is easy to see who the winner is here.

Saying positive things to yourself leads to having a positive attitude. Compliment yourself when you have done well. This type of attitude increases your chances of playing well and eventually increases your chances of winning. When you have a good attitude, you can feel good about yourself and win. Self-esteem, then, is one byproduct of a good attitude. When you act better, you feel good about yourself, you play better, and you do not take losing as seriously. Unfortunately, players at all levels tie self-esteem to wins and losses. When athletes lose, they often feel down on themselves. When they win, they feel good about themselves. The challenge is to separate the two. Losing a game does not make you a bad person. Parents and coaches need to reinforce this, and be positive in the face of a loss.

Parents play a crucial role in their young athlete's attitude. This begins by having parents who exhibit a positive attitude themselves. They do this by giving positive encouragement, praising their child whether he wins or loses, and displaying a calm demeanor in both victory and defeat. Children whose parents yell criticisms from the sidelines often do the same thing, yelling at their teammates, the officials, and their coaches. Likewise, when a parent has a positive attitude, this attitude is likely to trickle down to the child. He, too, will become more positive, encouraging, and full of self-esteem. This is the old "monkey-see, monkey-do" paradigm.

Parents can also help their child-athletes to develop a positive attitude by emphasizing effort and improvement more than winning and losing. They should also be careful to keep youth sports in perspective by realizing that it is a journey and not a destination with the understanding that, while kids understand winning and losing, they participate in sports mostly because they can be with their friends, develop their skills, and have fun. It is no fun for kids when the sport becomes something through which a parent or coach lives vicariously.

In my early tennis years, I was a perfectionist and very tough on myself. This perfectionism was positively reinforced because I was successful. Perhaps I thought being hard on myself helped me to win. Now I know that I could have won more easily and enjoyed playing more without the harsh, critical internal dialogue. When I won, I felt pretty good about myself. When I lost, I got way down on myself. My life was like a roller coaster—up when I won, down when I lost, up when I won again. I wish I had been a better partner to myself and savored my victories more.

Sports are not the only place where a positive attitude is important. The business world is full of stories about how a negative attitude did in an employee or ran a company into the ground. At work, negative people and negative environments can cause performance and health issues as well. In fact, studies have shown that people who maintain a positive attitude at work are promoted more quickly and become more successful.

Whether one is an executive or an employee, he cannot really be himself at work. The company and the employees depend on him to have a positive attitude and make the right choices for the company, the employees, and all concerned. We all carry our own psychological/emotional "baggage" to whatever we do. To assume that we can be who we are all of the time in the workplace is a dangerous misconception. As the Director of the Learning Center at Dean College, I approached every day and every decision I made with the idea that I was responsible to the college and the livelihood of my employees. I chose to create a positive work environment, not one operated on fear tactics. We had open lines of communication, and every decision I made was to empower my staff to perform their best. As a result of my mindset, both productivity and profitability in my area increased. If I had been "myself" every day I arrived at work, I would never have been able to accomplish what I did during the year I was there. The greatest achievement and compliment an executive or director or manager can receive is to significantly and positively impact productivity and to have her employees miss her when she is on vacation, be enthusiastic to go to work because of who she is, and never want her to leave the company. When I resigned my position at Dean College to return to the professional tennis tour, the president, Dr. Paula Rooney, told me that if I ever wanted to come back, that I was always welcome.

If you are an executive or manager who still thinks that having a negative attitude and being harsh and disrespectful produces the best results with your employees, think about it again. Employees have enough stress in their lives without their boss creating more. This type of approach will produce more illness and absenteeism, which negatively impacts the company's profitability. As an employee of a company, it is your responsibility to have a positive attitude, openly communicate in an effective manner, and to know and follow protocol, rules, and procedures that your company has in place. If an employee can easily receive compliments, then she is the ideal employee. Employees who thrive on negative feedback by creating "office foolishness" will always create situations in order to receive it. How can anyone create or be a part of a winning team if at the core of their being is the need to either be reprimanded or disruptive? This can only lead to a vicious cycle of non-productive behavior. This type of manager or employee wastes precious company time.

Bev worked for a decorating company in Bristol, Pennsylvania, and her mother, Anna Beck Gay, was her boss. Anna had a positive attitude, and she was a brilliant manager. She instilled in Bev and others to always treat everyone with respect and dignity. That was seen every day in her customer service skills and in how her employees wanted to do their best because of her. When employees are treated fairly and consistently, they will go the extra mile for their boss and the company. Anna had high expectations and required her employees to perform. It was the manner in which she managed that produced the results. She garnered respect and love from her employees. They wanted to come to work because she had created a fun, relaxed working atmosphere. To further illustrate her remarkable management skills, her husband John worked for her as well!

How many times have you heard someone say, "I have such a great boss?" Why can't everyone have a great boss? The skills to do this must be learned and practiced. Believe me, I know; I had to do that and I am glad that I did. Besides accomplishing what I did at Dean College, making these changes empowered me to be a better manager.

In the end, a few simple equations will show the impact of a positive attitude:

- Happy, positive thoughts = happy, positive events.

- Negative talk = more stress = more potential for injury or illness = non-optimal performance.

CHAPTER 11

MACH 4
MENTAL TRAINING SYSTEM™:
A HANDBOOK FOR ATHLETES, COACHES, AND PARENTS

The following text was taken from the MACH 4 Handbook.

The MACH 4 Mental Training System is a fun, fast, easy, effective way to teach athletes, coaches, and parents how to develop a prescription to win, increase self-esteem and confidence, control destructive emotions, learn dynamic strategies for creating a positive learning environment, find effective ways to reach their maximum potential, allow themselves to win, and develop healthy, positive relationships that foster a winning atmosphere. Why call the system MACH 4? There are four components: mental, body language, intensity level, and cueing language. Combining these four components will help anyone reach their goals "faster than the speed of sound." MACH 4 is unique because it teaches how to develop empowering relationships between parents, coaches, and players, and how to create a powerful partnership between the mind and the body by highlighting the mind/body connection, focusing on training the mind and the body at the same time, and integrating mental training into practice sessions. If athletes and coaches are looking for something to give them that added advantage, then MACH 4 may be the answer.

MACH 4 teaches much more than enhanced athletic performance. Life becomes easier, more rewarding, and more fun using the MACH 4 techniques. Everyone can learn how to empower themselves and others by creating the best win-win situations. Using the MACH 4 system, athletes learn how to maximize their performance in sports by relating to specific intensity levels and by managing destructive emotions like fear and anger. Winning can never be guaranteed, but we guarantee that if athletes practice using MACH 4 every day in and away from their athletic arena, they will enjoy life and competition more. They will be more successful in relationships and all endeavors that are important to them. Their life and performance will become easier and more fun.

MACH 4 teaches players how to manage their emotions, which will improve everything in their life. Every moment of the day, events occur where decisions must be made and interactions with others become critical. MACH 4 ensures the best results at all times. What one chooses to think in a moment, how one chooses to act in a moment, and what one chooses to say in a moment become defining. These three actions are all we really can control in our lives. Take the concepts from MACH 4, apply them not only to sports, but to relationships and life events, and you will be amazed at the positive results.

The mental part of sports is considered by most athletes and coaches to be at least 80–90%. Yet very few athletes and coaches take the time to train the mind at the same time they work on the physical skills of the game. If this mind/body training does not happen, how can the physical and the mental come together during competition? Mental training involves a coach educating his athletes; just like he teaches them technique, he can teach them mental skills to help them perform more easily and effortlessly with less chance of injury.

Most coaches only focus on technique and physical conditioning. Why not focus on creating mentally strong athletes who can perform when it counts? Mental training is the quickest way to improve performance. When players and coaches take responsibility for emotional and mental training, then they will have the complete package.

As an athlete, do you want to consistently perform your best, see immediate positive results, increase your confidence, control emotions that cause you to lose, be mentally and physically stronger, improve your concentration, and have fun and learn? As a coach, do you want to learn how to teach mental toughness skills, help your players perform better under pressure, become a better coach, integrate mental training into practice sessions, increase your player's self-esteem and confidence, identify thoughts and behaviors that hold your players back, manage team relationships, and improve team chemistry? If your answer is yes, then the MACH 4 Mental Training System is for you!

Since I started doing MACH 4 as a player, I have been able to play more easily and effortlessly with a faster recovery time. I also will not allow anyone on my team again who does not have a positive approach to my game. Since I started doing MACH 4 as a coach, I emphasize what a player is doing well, not constantly re-enforcing the word "mistake" to her mind because the mind will replicate what it is fed on a moment-to-moment daily basis. Children often put their coaches on a higher pedestal than even their parents. When I am coaching, I want to be the best role model that I can be. I know that what I say and do will either make or break a player's ability to become a stronger person and competitor. Is this not just as important and necessary as teaching the physical skills needed to compete and win? MACH 4 teaches this and much more.

Development of the MACH 4 System

Bev and I developed the MACH 4 Mental Training System as a result of my comeback beginning in January 2005. As Bev and I traveled to tournaments, it became more and more obvious to us the importance of the mental part of the game. When I first started back on tour, we focused on making some changes in my movement. But we soon realized that my mindset before, during, and after my matches was more important than the technical part of the game.

I was being featured in my singles matches, and I had not played on the tour for 14 years! I was *very* nervous, and I had no confidence in my game. Right before my match against Stephanie Dubois (ranked top 200 in the world) in Midland, Michigan, Bev said, "Just fake it." She told me to just act confidently, whether I felt confident or not, and to pretend that it did not bother me if I missed a shot. That was the beginning of the development of the MACH 4 system.

Bev has coached tennis for more than 25 years, so her expertise and positive approach to the game have helped me to be successful again on the tour. My new mental approach has helped me to improve more quickly and easily. I have incorporated the MACH 4 system into my current game, and it has dramatically improved my performance. Although I was the "guinea pig" for this system, Bev and I have also used it with club-level, Division I, world-ranked junior and tour players with fast and positive results. We believe this system can help players at all levels improve, and that these concepts can also be applied to other sports and professions.

The only things a player can absolutely control and be responsible for are what he thinks, how he acts, and what he says to himself and others when he steps onto the court or playing field. How many coaches and players integrate into practice sessions these important components, which can help them to maximize their performance? Most coaches emphasize technique, but how many incorporate simple mental techniques to help coach their players' minds to win? We have developed easy, fun and simple ways to coach the mind to win.

PRINCIPLES OF THE MACH 4 MENTAL TRAINING SYSTEM

The MACH 4 Mental Training System consists of mental, body language, intensity level, and cueing language components. All of these are interrelated and work together to create a positive partnership with the mind and the body to ensure maximum performance. In order to achieve this, the mind and the body have to be trained to work together as a team. Two of the seven principles of the MACH 4 system are as follows:

1. The system teaches that the mind controls the body. The mind tells the body what to

do and, in tennis, what shot to hit. The body cannot always execute the shot, but the mind is always in charge.

2. The system is easy to incorporate during on-court practice sessions. Each time a player steps onto the court for practice, she can work on her mental toughness skills.

COMPONENTS OF THE MACH 4 MENTAL TRAINING SYSTEM

The four components of the MACH 4 System and examples of each follow below.

MENTAL

The mind controls the body and tells it what to do. The mental part of tennis involves how an athlete thinks about his match before he walks onto the court; what he say to himself during the match; what he chooses to focus on during the match (execution and missed opportunities or what he is going to do on the next point); how he chooses to carry himself on the court; strategy and shot selection; reactions to missed shots, or a "blind" umpire or linesperson; maintaining his best intensity level; and what he and his coach choose to focus on after the match. The mental component of tennis—or any game that you play—is what you can say and do or think about to create the least amount of pressure on yourself so that you can perform.

Here is one example from the MACH 4 system of how to approach the mental part of the game:

THERE ARE NO MISTAKES—How many players have you watched who pay more attention to and expend more emotion on shots they miss than on shots they make? Too many players put a value judgment on their shots, particularly the ones they miss. By their reaction, one would sometimes think it was the end of the world when they miss a shot. The emotion that is attached to missing a shot reinforces the miss and causes a player to hold onto the miss longer than is necessary. When a player responds to a miss and not to those shots he hits well, he is reinforcing the negative instead of the positive; his mind will recreate the shots that he attached the most feeling to during the match. It is important to remember that there are no mistakes; a player either makes it or he misses it. Next time you miss, try saying to yourself, *No problem. I'll make the next one.* Next time you hit a winning shot, get excited and say to yourself, *Great shot. Way to go!*

Body Language

Body language will energize a player. From the moment a player arrives at a tennis tournament or competition, his body language—how he carries himself—is paramount. Does he project a confident, fighter image? Does he walk with a spring in his step, his head held high, and his shoulders back? How does he walk onto the court? A player can use his body language not only to intimidate his opponent before the competition even begins but to keep his own nerves at bay. That is the magic of MACH 4—no matter who the opponent is or how he is performing, you can project confidence with your own actions so that energy/intensity levels will remain strong and concentrated rather than being wasted or given away to your opponent. It is easy to do, and it is a choice. Try this experiment: sit in a chair, put your hands in your lap, drop your shoulders, and look down. You will feel your energy drop, too. Now, sit up tall with your shoulders back, head up, and look straight ahead. Can you feel the energy center in your chest just by making this simple adjustment?

During competition, it is critical to display powerful body language every moment of the match. For example, how a player walks between points, how she sits during a changeover, how she reacts to a missed shot, how she reacts to a well played point, and how she reacts to a winning shot. A player's body language should stay strong and confident no matter what is happening on the court. How many times have you seen a player allow her energy/intensity to drop after not executing a shot? How long will it take to restore the energy/intensity so that "free points" to an opponent are minimized and concentration is not disrupted? Why take the chance? If body language will easily help an athlete to be able to sustain positive emotions and energy and concentration, then why not practice it and use it to win?

In developing the body language components of the MACH 4 System, Bev and I have borrowed some terms and concepts from the martial arts. The same types of philosophies that students use in tae kwon do or karate can be applied to tennis and all other sports. Here is one example of body language that a player can use to immediately improve her performance.

ACT CONFIDENT (OR JUST FAKE IT)—
Most players do not think about it, but acting confident is so important. Would you rather play against someone who walks around the court

calmly, confidently, and in control, or someone who gets angry, throws her racquet, and shares a constant, negative dialogue about how badly she is playing? It is much more intimidating to play against someone who is in control of her emotions and projects calmness and confidence. During a match, confidence can come and go, so whenever you are not feeling it, fake it—act as if you are confident. This will help keep your shots strong and prevent your opponent from knowing how you feel.

INTENSITY LEVEL

It is so important to recognize physical responses to match moments. Intensity level has to do with not only a physical feeling but also with footwork and how hard a player swings at the ball. A drop in intensity of just 10% will affect results. For example, if a player is serving for the match and her intensity level decreases, it is very likely that she will not perform her best that game. Most tennis players have a tendency to slow down their hand on the serve at important times during matches. This is a decrease in intensity. When a player slows her hand down on her serve, the pace of her serve decreases and this gives her opponent the opportunity to hit a better return. It is possible to have too high of an intensity level as well. What if a player swings too hard at the serve, causing the ball to sail long?

In the MACH 4 system, we rate intensity level on a scale from 1–5. In this system, 1–2 = low intensity; 3–4 = medium intensity; and 5 = high intensity. When a player is swinging at the ball with her intensity level at 1 or 2, she will not win many points. When a player is swinging at the ball with her intensity level at 5, she will either be exhausted by the third or fourth game of the match, or she will be missing so many shots that she will lose quickly. We coach our players to swing at the ball with a 3 or 4 intensity level and on some shots with a 5 intensity level. We do not recommend using a 5 intensity level on match point! Remember to individualize this to your player's style and technique. A level 4 on one player's serve will be different than a level 4 on another player's serve.

Cueing Language

Cueing is a term that has been used in the aerobics industry. Bev and I have found cueing to be helpful not only with my own tennis, but with players we teach at all levels of the game. It also adds humor to practices. When players are less intense, their muscles remain more relaxed, which helps them execute their shots.

Cues are words or phrases that can trigger certain mental, emotional, visual, and physical responses. Cueing can and should also be individualized. A cue or term that works for one player might not work for another. It is important for coaches and players to come up with cues that are meaningful for them.

Bev and I have coined certain terms and phrases that are descriptive of specific shots and situations. We first teach the technique involved in the shot. Then, when the player understands the physical way to hit the shot, we only need to cue her with a word or phrase. It helps keep things simple and fun.

Martina Navratilova loved the cueing I used when I coached her during the 2005 WTT Boston Lobsters season. Hey, if it is good enough for Martina, it is good enough for the rest of us! The example of cueing language below, First Strike, is one of Martina's favorites.

FIRST STRIKE—Martina loved this phrase, and it helped her to win a pivotal match for the Boston Lobsters against the New York

Sportimes that put us into the playoffs. Martina was playing against Jenny Hopkins, a very good player ranked in the top 150 in the world. Jenny was running Martina all over the court. I knew it was in Martina's best interest to end the points as quickly as possible, rather than getting into long rallies. One of Martina's best combos is her return of serve and coming in behind it to volley. I told her to do first strike. She said, "What's first strike?" I quickly told her to get "Jenny running before Jenny gets you running. Take the first ball and make an aggressive shot. Hit this next return down the line and come into the net." Martina caught on quickly (she is, of course, very smart!) and she ended up beating Jenny.

MACH 4 POINT SYSTEM

MACH 4 is not only for improving on-court behavior but improving off-court behavior as well. We have created a daily point and bonus point system using MACH 4 components of body language and intensity. We also use it to train certain off-court behaviors, or actions, as well. The bonus point system incorporates MACH 4 with off-court behaviors such as saying "please" and "thank you," picking up after yourself, being kind to one another, following rules, picking up balls without being asked, following your nutrition plan, etc. This point system has been effective with the players we coach because they are so competitive.

Mach 4 has quickly improved their behavior, raised their self-esteem, and elevated their level of play. The best testimony is from the players. They play with less fear and better results. Here are some comments from world ranked junior players about how MACH 4 has helped them both on and off the court:

- "Mach 4 helps me to control my emotions and to concentrate on the court when I am playing. It has helped me to know when I need to raise my energy in matches and how to act like a champion. I have started to feel myself stronger on the court. Mach 4 has also helped me in my life. I am now nicer to the people who are around me."

"When I first started to learn and use Mach 4, I knew it would help me so much. I know emotional control is very important in tennis and in life. Mach 4 has helped me be a stronger player. It has also helped me be a good person with others. When there is respect in communication, there are fewer misunderstandings with each other. Mach 4 helps me live easy."

CONCLUSION

MACH 4 positively impacts behaviors both on and off the court. It is more than just about tennis or competition; it makes a difference in people's lives. MACH 4 helps people become better people. It helps build respect, increase emotional control, improve communication, increase self-discipline, and create better relationships.

The MACH 4 Mental Training System can be used in any sport. I have focused on tennis, but the same philosophy and concepts can be applied to football, baseball, basketball, golf, swimming or any other sport that you play or coach. Athletic competition often comes down to moments. MACH 4 connects the physical conditioning and technique with the mind to maximize an athlete's performance. MACH 4 gives your player or child the mental edge to win.

GOD AND CHUNKY MONKEY

Teamwork, respect, attitude, fun, and mental conditioning are all universal keys to winning in sports, business, and life. I have found a few other things that have helped me to be successful and win in my recent comeback in professional tennis. For me, a new spirituality, physical conditioning, and better nutrition habits are essential for my mind and body to perform at their best. Besides being helpful in athletic competition and business, these components have transformed my life.

CHUNKY MONKEY

I love to eat. As one of my friends says, "You're a good little eater!" Since leaving the pro tour in 1991, I have continually struggled with the ups and downs of weight management and fitness. Some years have been better than others. Most of the time I would take the easy way out and buy bigger pants! But, my mindset has changed. I have finally settled on a lifestyle plan that works for me. As I have learned how to manage my emotions — not deny them — proper nutrition and exercise have become my friend, not my worst enemy. My favorite food is Mexican, and I do love chocolate as well. I recently discovered the Ben & Jerry's ice cream flavor called Chunky Monkey. It is the best. Is it possible to eat these types of foods and make my comeback? Yes—within reason. I have tried many diets. I had no energy on the popular fat diet. So when Bev, who was on a low fat diet due to a medical condition, told me the cellulite on her legs had "disappeared", I decided to try a modified version.

Of course, I could never do a low-fat diet, but I do limit my caloric intake—and it has worked really well for me. I have lost inches and body fat as well. My family was "shocked" when they saw me recently for an event in Dallas. I eat six small meals a day, and I have plenty of energy for what I am doing. I can no longer eat bags of M&Ms, but I can eat a small amount of M&Ms as long as I factor this into my specified calories per day plan. It is amazing what one can become used to when she puts her mind to it. I am also doing MACH 4 and coaching my mind to think of it as an eating lifestyle plan rather than a diet. For me, just thinking about the word "diet" hindered me from being able to sustain it as part of my life. My mother was so impressed with how I looked that she asked me to send her a sample of what I have been doing. Please remember that I am not a nutritionist or a physical trainer; I have included a sample below to demonstrate what has worked for me.

MACH 4
MENTAL TRAINING SYSTEM™
EATING AND EXERCISE
LIFESTYLE PLAN

TIPS TO FOLLOW THE PLAN:

1. This is an eating lifestyle plan; it is a way of living. It is not a "diet."

2. Eat six small meals a day—eat one meal approximately every three hours.

3. Schedule your meals—eat at approximately (within 15 minutes) the same time every day.

4. Base your caloric intake on this simple formula: total number of current caloric intake - 500 calories. If you are eating 3000

calories a day, start eating 2500 calories a day and gradually decrease your number of calories to about 1800 a day and limit your fat intake to 35 grams or less a day (like me!).

5. Keep a daily journal of your meals, including type of food and calories.

6. When you eat out, eat your specified portion and take the rest home.

7. For the sweet tooth in you: eat chocolate for one of your snacks.

8. Stick with it—this eating and exercise lifestyle plan will get easier the more you practice it.

9. If you get off of the plan for a day, get right back on it the next day. No one is perfect!

10. When you reach your best "look" according to your age, stop losing weight and just maintain.

EXAMPLE OF ONE DAY IN THE LIFE OF ANNE'S EATING AND EXERCISE LIFESTYLE PLAN (BASED ON 1750 CALORIES):

Breakfast—8am—400 calories (Bran flakes with 1% milk and ½ bagel)

Morning snack—11am—200 calories (banana, slice of raisin bread or ½ bagel)

Lunch—1pm—350 calories (tuna sandwich on wheat, piece of fruit)

Afternoon snack—4pm—200 calories (1/4 cup of M&Ms)

Dinner—6:30pm—400 calories (chicken breast, broccoli with sautéed garlic, red potatoes)

Evening snack—9:30pm—200 calories (tortilla with cheese and hot sauce or ½ bagel)

I like Thomas' New York-style bagels and frozen dinners by Smart Ones. You can eat what you want, crave, like, and enjoy within the specified calories.

2:00 pm—I exercise 30 minutes five times a week. I walk on the treadmill for ten minutes and then do a series of exercises for my legs, arms/shoulders, and stomach. Then I stretch. It is important to schedule your exercise for approximately the same time of day so that it becomes part of your routine.

There is no substitute in life for good health. If we do not maintain our car, we can trade it in or buy a new one. We only get one body to carry us through this lifetime. Take care of it!

GOD KNOWS BEST

I now remind myself all the time that God knows best. For more than 43 years, I wanted to be in control of everything and force things to happen. Just ask my parents! Now, I just pray. I pray about everything, and I ask God to show me His Divine Plan for my life. I ask Him to guide me and to make it obvious what I need to do each day.

With God in charge, my life is so much more exciting and fun. I cannot even imagine the things that God has in store for me. Thinking that I could control everything in relationships and in business was not effective for me. It just made things more difficult and disappointing. Now, I go with the flow and ask God to provide me with opportunities and "open doors." What he has in store for me is limitless, whereas my own thinking as a human being is limited. In other words, I do not put parameters or restrictions around what I might be able to achieve with God's help.

I believe that everything happens for a reason; there are no mistakes or coincidences. The writings of Florence Scovel Shinn, an early twentieth-century "success" teacher and metaphysician, have impacted my life. What she said about the power of the spoken word and thoughts is so true: whatever I choose to think about will eventually happen in my life. So now I am much more mindful of how powerful my thoughts, words, and actions are. I do not allow myself to entertain negative thinking as I did before. Negative thinking colors everything, especially how you perceive your environment and what you allow into your life. It can sometimes even be a matter of life and death. Bev credits author and metaphysical lecturer, Louise L. Hay, for her miraculous cure of a rare hereditary blood disorder that occurred in December 1990. Every day during the year she battled that illness, she listened to Ms. Hay's subliminal tape with healing affirmations. In December 1991, she experienced an "instantaneous healing" and knew in that moment that the disease was gone. Her doctor at Massachusetts General Hospital in Boston called it a medical miracle. In November 2004, 14 years later, the blood disorder returned. She once again beat the odds when in June 2005; she "felt" her body "shift" once again. Blood tests confirmed that the illness had once again gone away. In fact, her blood counts are the best they have ever been in her life. There is no quantifiable explanation for the remission. For Bev, it is a matter of life or death what her mindset is moment to moment. There is no place in her life for strong, negative thoughts, emotions, or behavior. It is not worth the risk. She very much understands how fragile and precious life is on this earth and how the power of the mind can both heal and help to maintain stronger health.

So, how do I proceed about letting God be in charge? Well, as I said, I pray about everything. Every morning during my car ride and at different times during the day, I pray. I always begin by asking God to protect me and my family, and then I go into specifics. It is amazing the difference this has made in my life. Opportunities come to me now. I do not have to force things to happen, and when I do, I catch myself and stop. Praying and managing my own emotions has enabled me to have "two-way" communication - my intuition gets stronger every day. This has enabled me to be more creative, take more risks, and make better choices, which is critical in all aspects of life. Even Donald Trump believes in the importance of intuition in business. "You may have the academic credentials, but without instincts you'll have a hard time getting to - and staying at - the top," Trump says. Praying has been a way for me to develop my intuition. It has "led" me to do certain things. For example, I prayed to be the coach of the Boston Lobsters professional tennis team. On a flight back to Boston after the 2004 U.S. Open, my seat on the plane "happened" to be directly in front of the future owner of the Boston Lobsters, Bahar Uttam. I "happened," for the first time, to put on a t-shirt that morning with my name on the back featuring a Grand Slam team clinic that I had run in Boston. For anyone who knows me, it was very unusual for me to wear a shirt with my name on it. Bahar saw my name and remembered that we had previously met at a tennis event. This chance meeting led to a wonderful friendship as well as a great business relationship. I will never forget the feeling that I had when Bahar asked me to coach the new Boston Lobsters. My prayers were answered!

I prayed to be healthy and play on the women's professional tennis tour again. I am now playing competitive professional tennis. I prayed for the opportunity to give presentations at tennis conferences, and now I am doing so. I know God will only answer those prayers that will be the best for me. How often have you wanted to see a job, a relationship, or event happen, only to see later that it would not have been the best thing for you? Disappointment then turns to relief knowing that potential disasters were avoided and that greater things were accomplished that were not even imagined.

The other thing I do is to think about and imagine what I want to have happen in my life. For example, I want to be able to tour the country, giving talks and presentations about the material in this book. If that is what is best for me, God will provide the way. Whatever you think about and dwell upon will happen in your life. That is why I do not permit myself to get down in the dumps or to think negatively very long because I have experienced what that can bring into my life. This positive way of thinking and being is also helping me to enjoy each day rather than always looking to the past or the future.

This approach may seem a little radical since I was brought up in a Christian home and our family attended a Baptist church. I have always had a connection to God, but I thought about Him much differently growing up than I do now. The writings of Emmet Fox, whose work is based on spirituality, positive thinking, and a literal interpretation of the Bible, have also impacted me. In one of his books, he breaks down the Lord's Prayer and talks about each stanza. It is a wonderful way to think about God. Take the first line—"Our Father who art in Heaven"—which I think is really incredible. God is my Father, not my taskmaster. He is there to help me not to punish me. This change in my thinking has brought me closer to others and the realization of how important joy is in my daily life.

Unfortunately, some people, in the name of their religion, are often self-righteous and judgmental toward others in the world. I often wonder how all that started. It is not anyone's place to judge another, yet we are all guilty of this. I love to listen to Houston's "Smiling Preacher," Joel Osteen. His uplifting, positive, humorous messages are certainly refreshing. Those of you who are Christian know that Jesus asked us to judge no one and to simply love others as we love ourselves. As we all learn to love ourselves more, there is so much more that we can achieve. God's grace and love are what I focus on. As I said before, my God is not a harsh God, and this realization has helped to transform my life.

Bev and I have also created a team of those we love who have passed on to that other life that we cannot see. There is nothing harder to reconcile than losing someone you love. When my brother Roy died, I was crushed. A family friend flew in from Dallas to tell me. When she first walked through the door, I obviously knew something was wrong. My initial thought was that my dad had a heart attack. When she told me that Roy had taken his life, I let out a guttural scream—something from the core of me. I was beyond shocked. I had not seen it coming at all. I was devastated. At the time this happened, I was taking classes and coaching at Trinity University. It was weird because I had this feeling that something was seriously wrong. As I was walking across campus that day toward the library, a sense of doom came over me. So by the time Mrs. Cole walked through my apartment door, I knew something awful had happened.

I flew home that night. I do not know how my parents survived his death. Actually, I do know—it is their faith. Otherwise, his death would have probably kept them torn apart inside and sent them into a despair that is difficult to overcome. My way of coping was to go back to Trinity and bury myself in my studies. I made the Dean's List that semester—my first and only time to do that. At the writing of this book, it has been over 20 years since his death, but sometimes it feels like yesterday. I have never gotten over it, and I never will. It is not something you *can* get over.

You think back about what you could have done, what you did not do, how you did not even know or see it coming. When I stop and think about him, it is still so painful I can hardly stand it. That is probably why I did not stop moving and doing. That was my way of coping with it. Since I have tuned in more to metaphysics and the other plane, I know that Roy is helping me and guiding me. This does help, but the pain never goes away.

For me the moral of this story is that bad things happen, things that you never recover from, but you must keep going. We have to because if we do not, we will die too, if not physically, then emotionally and spiritually. We must keep looking forward, not back at events that we cannot change.

Recently, Bev and I watched Susan St. James and her family talk on the Oprah Winfrey Show about the tragic death of their son and brother, Teddy. Bev said she could "see" Teddy right up there, smiling, next to them. I did not doubt it for a second. We choose to believe that those who have passed on have not left us. In fact, they are very willing to help—if we ask. They make themselves known to us through "signs" that we look for every day. Bev has developed a system using the numbers and letters on license plates to "communicate" with her beloved parents. It is truly remarkable to witness this every day and realize how much help we now receive. Knowing that we are protected and guided by God and all those who love us is such an incredible comfort as we face the challenges of each day. This belief has certainly helped us to understand and live each day easier knowing how much God and our loved ones continue to protect, guide, and care about us.

Conclusion

The themes that I have covered in this book are guidelines for helping you to win in sports, business, and life. They are intended to guide you as a player, coach, manager, employee, parent— and most importantly as a person. It is up to you to use them as you feel appropriate and to decide which are the most important in your quest to empower yourself and others.

Competition is the lifeblood of our existence. It furthers us both personally and professionally, and creates a healthy environment in which we can grow and learn. However, we all know that competition practiced unfairly is not healthy and, at times, even dangerous, both physically and emotionally. True winners understand the spirit of competition and what it embodies. Victory is never guaranteed, and the score is not all that matters. Someone once said that winning is a byproduct of how you play the game. I hope that I have helped you to understand what it takes to "play the game" and that you, too, are a "Grand Slam" winner in all that is important to you.

ABOUT THE AUTHOR

Anne Smith, Ph.D., won her place in the history books of all-time winners with ten Grand Slam championships in doubles and mixed doubles from 1980 to 1984. She is one of only 20 women in the history of the Open Era of tennis (1968 to present) who have won ten or more Grand Slam titles, and one of only 13 women in the Open Era to complete a career Grand Slam in women's doubles by winning at least one doubles title at all four of the majors. She has won three US Open titles, two Wimbledon titles, four French Open titles, and one Australian Open title. She has been a member of the Wightman Cup and Federation Cup teams. She was ranked No. 1 in the world in doubles in 1980 and 1981, and reached a career-high No.12 in singles in 1982. Anne was a member of three World TeamTennis Championship Teams—the Boston Lobsters, the San Antonio Racquets, and the Dallas Stars. She went on to win the 35-and-over women's doubles at the U.S. Open and Wimbledon in 1997.

As a junior, Anne was No. 1 in Texas from the 12s through the 18s. When she was 15, she was No. 1 in Texas in both 16 and 18 singles. At age 17, Anne went to Paris and became the first American to win the French Open Junior Singles Championship. She holds 21 national junior and adult titles. In Texas, Anne was awarded the coveted Mary Lowden Award for sportsmanship four years in a row from 1974–1977. She also received the Maureen Connolly Brinker award in 1977 for the most outstanding full season performance in the 18-and-under division in the U.S. Anne was born and raised in Dallas, Texas, and has been inducted into the Texas Tennis Hall of Fame.

After her active tennis career, Anne returned to Trinity University and earned her Bachelor's degree. She then enrolled at the University of Texas at Austin where she completed her doctorate in Educational Psychology with a specialty in School Psychology. She is licensed to practice in Arizona, Texas, and Massachusetts. Anne practiced school psychology in the Judson Independent School District in San Antonio,

Texas, before moving to Boston, where she was the Director of the Learning Center for Dean College in Franklin, Massachusetts. She recently moved to Phoenix, where she is practicing psychology in the schools and coaching. Anne still maintains her Boston connection, where she is the Coach of the World TeamTennis Boston Lobsters and the mental training consultant for Harvard University's women's tennis team. The Lobsters reached the playoffs as a first-year franchise, and Harvard became the first Ivy League school to be ranked nationally in the Top ten. She is a USPTA Pro 1 and a member of the Head/Penn Racquet Sports Speaker's Bureau.

Anne is playing on the women's tour again at the age of 46. She began her comeback in January 2005. After only nine tournaments, she has reached the semi-finals in doubles four times, and she won her first doubles tour title in June 2005, after being off the tour for 14 years.

To contact Anne for further information about her books or to schedule her for a presentation to your team, school, or company, you may contact her by phone at 480-272-5085 or by email at anne@annesmithtennis.com.

www.ingramcontent.com/pod-product-compliance
Lightning Source LLC
Chambersburg PA
CBHW021332090426
42742CB00008B/578